MW01108292

Songs

FOR YOUR PATH

A Daily Devotional from the Book of Psalms

BY C.J. HARRIS

PositiveAction
BIBLE CURRICULUM

Songs for Your Path

By C.J. Harris

Copyright © 2016 by Positive Action for Christ, Inc. P.O. Box 700, 502 W. Pippen
Street, Whitakers, NC 27891.

All rights reserved. No part may be reproduced in any manner without permission
in writing from the publisher.

Scripture quotations taken from King James Version.

First printing.

Printed in the United States of America

ISBN: 978-1-59557-198-4

Edited by Christa Lord
Layout and Design by Shannon Brown

Published by

Preface

T he book you hold in your hands grew out of my personal journey through the Book of Psalms. Recorded in these pages are snapshots of God's revealed glory, the wisdom for righteousness, and the joy found in the presence of our Father.

The Jews place this book in the same category as Proverbs, Job, and Ecclesiastes. Above all, the Psalms are meant to teach their reader wisdom—how to live in light of God's character and within the order of His creation. Think of Psalms as a map to blessing both now and for all eternity. Each song and poem is a signpost, pointing us to God and to the path He has lain out for His people.

I pray that your journey is as uplifting and edifying as mine. And I trust you will finish with a song of praise on your lips.

By His grace,

C. J. Harris
Rocky Mount, North Carolina

A Call to God's Path

Psalm 1:1

"Blessed is the man that walketh not in the counsel of the ungodly, nor standeth in the way of sinners, nor sitteth in the seat of the scornful."

The Book of Psalms presents its reader with two ways in this world. The first is the way of the godly—those who have made God their first and highest pursuit. This path is lined with blessing, hope, joy, wisdom, and all that is truly good. But it is not an easy path, for there is much opposition. Yet it is the only path that leads to the One for whom we were all created.

The second path is the path of the ungodly, or those who have chosen anything other than God as their ultimate pursuit. Christ calls this path the way of destruction (Matt. 7:13). Much travel has worn this path smooth, which makes for easy going. Its travelers will also find many companions to encourage and help them along the way. Psalms names many of these companions—the fool, the wicked, the scoffer, and the liar, to mention a few.

The psalmists call us to the godly path, echoing the call in Proverbs: understand the fear of the Lord, and find the knowledge of God (Prov. 2:5). These poets and songwriters describe the glory of the God of our way; they fight off attacks along the path; and they plead with wayward pilgrims to rejoin the King's road.

Final Thought: Only two paths lead through this life. Where is yours heading?

The Delight of the Path

Psalm 1:2

"But his delight is in the law of the LORD; and in his law doth he meditate day and night."

It's been said that the most important part of a trip is not the destination, but the journey itself. When I was a child traveling with my family, I would take along a book to read on the road. My dad would inevitably glance in the rearview mirror, and seeing my nose buried in the book, he would tell me to put the book down and look at the scenery. He believed that the journey was just as important as the destination.

The psalmist shared my dad's love for the journey, but on an entirely different level. As we follow the path of God, He is our destination. After all, who wouldn't look forward to an eternity in heaven with Him?

But God is also the joy along the path. We can delight in Him as we meditate in the Word. Too many of us become so focused on heaven that we fail to realize that God wants us to begin heavenly worship in this life. He has given us an entire book—66 books, actually—to help us know, love, and praise His name right now.

And this worship isn't confined to church services or devotional times. The delight is available day and night, without end, all along our winding, narrow way. We can taste it in His creation; we can share it in fellowship with His people; we can experience it during acts of service for His glory; and we can even find it simply by being still and knowing that He is our God. The way of God is a way of true delight.

Final Thought: Take time to delight in God today.

The Fruit of the Path

Psalm 1:3

"And he shall be like a tree planted by the rivers of water, that bringeth forth his fruit in his season; his leaf also shall not wither; and whatsoever he doeth shall prosper."

Robert Frost ended one of his best-known poems with the following lines:

> *Two roads diverged in a wood, and I—*
> *I took the one less traveled by,*
> *And that has made all the difference.*

Similarly, Psalm 1 concludes its song of the two ways by presenting where each will lead. Though every path has its own unique twists and turns, ups and downs, valleys and vistas—the path of God will always lead to spiritual life and blessing, while the paths of this world plunge travelers into death and destruction.

The Psalmist uses a second image to describe the person that delights in the Lord and His Law, comparing him with a tree rooted deeply into the bank of a river. As he abides there, his life bears fruit in God-appointed seasons.

The picture here brings to mind the fruit of the Spirit (Gal. 5:22–23) and the fruit of righteousness (Phil. 1:9–11), both of which grow by the inward work of Christ for God's glory. God preserves this tree from destruction, and its leaves do not wither. So long as the tree draws life from the River, it will bear fruit. And as believers follow God's path, His grace will lead them home.

The wicked find none of this blessing on their path (Ps. 1:4–6). None of their labors produce lasting fruit, but rather chaff, the empty husks left after the good seed is gleaned, which the winds of time and circumstance drive away. These people will also pass before the Lord, but they will not stand before His judgment. Their path will lead to the destruction of their lives and all their works.

Final Thought: Pursue God above all else, and you will rejoice to see His fruit in your life.

The Unopposable Lord

Psalm 2:4

"He that sitteth in the heavens shall laugh: the LORD shall have them in derision."

Now, as ever, so many people rail against God. In the media, public figures ignore or attack His moral law. In academia, teachers deny the truth of His Word. In churches, preachers and theologians dilute or abuse Scripture. And all this just inside the western world—outside, God's people face persecution, imprisonment, and even death.

In short, humankind wages constant warfare against God. But does this worry Him? Is He troubled by what seems like an ever-growing opposition?

On the contrary, the Lord sits on His throne in heaven and laughs at these fruitless efforts. The psalmist goes so far as to say that God derides the wicked schemers of this world. He is merely allowing the cup of His wrath to fill to the brim (Rev. 16:19).

We shouldn't complain that God delays His judgment. His patience, after all, has given you and me time to repent from our sin and turn to Christ. We should be grateful for the mercy God shows when humankind rejects Him, because each of us has turned away from God at some point.

But know that God will one day judge those who choose to oppose Him.

Christian, does the seeming might of the wicked burden you? Do you fear the attacks from your culture, your community, or even your church?

This song of the King calls you to lay such fears at the foot of God's throne. Rest in His power and trust in His plan. Pray along with Maltbie Babcock,

> *This is my Father's world.*
> *O let me ne'er forget*
> *That though the wrong*
> *Seems oft so strong,*
> *God is the ruler yet.*

Final Thought: Our God reigns omnipotent, and none can overthrow Him.

Submission Is Wisdom

Psalm 2:11

"Serve the LORD with fear, and rejoice with trembling."

At the heart of wisdom is the ability to make right judgments. For this reason, the Bible points out that folly is bound up in a child's heart. The young boy thinks to himself, "Jumping down three steps is fun and easy. I'll try eight next time." He lacks the judgment to foresee the disastrous outcome of his decisions. As an adult, he gains wisdom from experience and observation, which replace much of this juvenile thinking.

The second psalm concludes with a call to wisdom. The Father has given His Son dominion over every nation and every land (v. 8). As ruler, the Son will crush all enemies with a rod of iron (v. 9). He will overthrow all opposition. In light of such power, rebellion is mere folly. Wisdom dictates submission and reverence.

Sadly, many still respond to the Son's rule with foolish defiance. Yet those who refuse to submit will perish from the way (v. 12). They will come under the wrath of the King they have rejected. But those who choose to submit in faith will find only blessing. God's people will rejoice in the eternal favor of their King.

Final Thought: Submission to God brings joy and blessing. Be wise.

Rest in God During Trials

Psalm 3:5

"I laid me down and slept; I awaked; for the LORD sustained me."

In this psalm about trials, verse five seems a bit out of place. David looks around him and finds enemies on every side. They mock him and his faith, saying David's hope in God is useless. "Give up your hope, and tremble in fear!" they shout.

Like David's enemies, trials can challenge the hope and peace we have in God. We're tempted to think that our situation is never going to get any better. We'll never get past this struggle, so we may as well give up. It's natural to react to problems with fear and worry—for many people, anxiety regularly fills their day and robs them of sleep at night.

But a believer doesn't need to respond to trials that way. David reminds us that all believers have an escape from fear and worry—hope in God. We can cry out to the Lord in our troubles, and like a caring father, He will hear us and come to our aid.

Life will always bring difficult trials, but we rest secure in a God who knows our struggles, hears our prayers, and answers in love. We can lie down and sleep in peace.

Final Thought: God will give you peace as you rest in Him.

More Joy than a Feast

Psalm 4:7

"Thou hast put gladness in my heart, more than in the time that their corn and their wine increased."

For those of us who have food readily available in the form of all-you-can-eat buffets and well-stocked grocery stores, it's difficult to appreciate the joy of a true harvest feast. We can find fresh food easily, but most people in earlier centuries didn't have this luxury. For them, meal options included seasonal crops or preserved food. When harvest came—the time when laborers gathered fresh, plentiful food—it brought great rejoicing.

The Jewish celebration of harvest began with the Feast of First Fruits and culminated seven weeks later with the Feast of Weeks, also called Pentecost.

After harvesting the barley and wheat crops, the Israelites gathered in Jerusalem to thank the Lord for His provision. Rejoicing echoed through the city as the smells of freshly baked bread drifted through the air. Grape harvest began soon after the feasts, so people brought out the rest of the previous year's wine. If the grain harvest and the previous grape harvest had been plentiful, there would be even greater festivity.

David, surveying all this merriment, makes a passionate statement—in God, he finds more joy than in the abundance of harvest. The feasting satisfies for a moment, but the joy of God runs deeper and longer than any outward pleasure.

The nineteenth-century hymn writer, Fanny Crosby, conveys a similar thought in her hymn, "Take the World, But Give Me Jesus."

> *Take the world, but give me Jesus,*
> *All its joys are but a name;*
> *But His love abideth ever,*
> *Through eternal years the same.*

Final Thought: No joy of this life can compare to the joy found in God. Where is your joy found?

A Prayer for Straight Paths

Psalm 5:8

"Lead me, O LORD, in thy righteousness because of mine enemies; make thy way straight before my face."

No one can follow God's way in his or her own strength. The enemies without and within pull us back toward the path of the wicked and its destructive end. Only the One who built the path of righteousness can keep pilgrims upon it.

David recognized this fact and prayed to the Lord of the path for clarity. He desired God's guidance. The paths of the world twist and turn, easily misleading the most diligent pilgrim. Knowing this, David prayed that God would make the path straight before him, making the right way so clear that he could not miss it.

Like David, we must call on God to guide us. On every side, voices call us to side paths with enticing words and worldly wisdom. The simplicity of the straight path can be obscured when we turn to sources other than God's Word for guidance. God doesn't author such confusion. God makes the path plain as we prayerfully wait upon Him.

Final Thought: Seek God's grace to walk the path of righteousness.

God's Mercy on the Weak

Psalm 6:4

"Return, O LORD, deliver my soul: oh save me for thy mercies' sake."

As Jesus preached the Sermon on the Mount, He began with the words, "Blessed are the poor in spirit" (Matt. 5:3). In presenting His kingdom, Jesus wanted His hearers to know that it was peopled by the weak. Its citizens knew they had no spiritual wealth to buy God's favor. All who come to God come empty-handed.

When we request God's forgiveness, we have nothing with which to commend ourselves to God. Our sin and its fruits of sorrow, pain, and frustration belong to us. We have no righteousness of our own to remove it. Nor can we borrow righteousness from others, for all of humanity are spiritual paupers. And no work we do can make amends for our sin against God. Forgiveness comes only by God's loving mercy—freely given in Christ.

God will answer our prayers for forgiveness. He will restore us as a father restores repentant children. The wrath we deserve has already been poured out on Christ, without a drop remaining for us. For this reason we can pray in full confidence of God's mercy.

Final Thought: In Christ, we find mercy and forgiveness.

The Need for Repentance

Psalm 7:12

"If he turn not, he will whet his sword; he hath bent his bow, and made it ready."

We enter this world on the wrong path. Our nature predisposes us to seek our own good and our own pleasure, leading us in ways of sin and self-righteousness. This nature is so ingrained that David declared that we wander astray from our mother's womb (Ps. 58:3). We all begin on the path of destruction.

With such inauspicious beginnings, our only hope rests in God's longsuffering mercy. We deserve wrath, but God gives time to repent (Rom. 2:4). He gave us the Word and even His own Son to call us away from destruction. If we will repent and believe, God promises to put us on the path of life.

The danger lies in mistaking God's forbearance for disinterest. Since God delays judgment, some wrongly assume that God will not judge or that He doesn't care. David corrects this error by picturing God ready to strike those who refuse to repent. He stands with sword sharpened and bow bent (v. 12). The weapons of war are prepared, and the arrow is trained on its target (v. 13). To go on in our natural way will bring doom, but if we turn back to God in repentance, there is a sure hope.

Final Thought: If you would come to Christ, you must repent.

The Eminence of God's Glory

Psalm 8:1

"O LORD, our Lord, how excellent is thy name in all the earth! Who hast set thy glory above the heavens."

As we follow God's path, our focus turns naturally to Him. His blazing glory far surpasses the beauty of heaven and Earth. Those who walk the world's path recognize God's majesty, but they must be content seeing it only in Earth's dim reflection.

The exact size of the universe is immeasurable, and its immensity reminds us of Earth's smallness and insignificance. We even have trouble comprehending the distances that we can measure. To cover the distance across our own galaxy, the Milky Way, would take 100,000 years at light speed—that is, over one thousand lifetimes. That God pays attention to us should direct our focus onto Him, with gratitude and dependence.

In addition to His creation, God also draws attention to His glory by working through weak things to overcome the mighty (1 Cor. 1:26–29). He uses the foolish to shame the wise. God's repeated use of the overlooked leaves the wicked perplexed and brings them to acknowledge God's glory, if only for a brief time (Ps. 8:2). God uses all of creation—including the weak things in it—to exalt His glory to all.

Final Thought: Oh Lord, how excellent is Your name in all the earth!

God's People Sing

Psalm 9:1

"I will praise thee, O LORD, with my whole heart; I will shew forth all thy marvellous works."

God's path rings with the praises of His saints. Christian history is filled with songs, poems, and hymns composed by the followers of Christ. In this psalm, David shows a whole-hearted desire to praise God in word and song. He sings of both God's works (v. 1) and character (v. 2).

Songs of praise reverberate throughout Scripture. The Book of Job—one of the oldest portions of the Old Testament—is written as an epic poem. In it, we learn that the angels sang and shouted for joy when God created the earth (Job 38:7). Moses sang God's praises at the destruction of Pharaoh's army (Exo. 15). David, Aseph, and Solomon all poured out poetry and song in their writings. In the New Testament, Paul pens an early Christian hymn in his letter to the Ephesian church (Eph. 1:1–14). In the Revelation, John gives us a preview of the singing in heaven (Rev. 5:9–10).

God's people continued to sing throughout the early church age. In the second century, the Christian author Tertullian stated that the singing of Psalms is an essential part of church worship. Other notable Christians of the time—such as Athanasis of Alexandria, Eusebius of Caesaria, and Basil the Great—also shared this belief.

The Reformation era saw an explosion of new hymns and songs as the Reformers praised God, taught doctrine, and celebrated their freedom in Christ. More songs were written during periods of revival in following centuries, adding to this rich musical heritage. Today, God's people continue to praise Him by creating still more poetry and song. As we walk the Lord's path, let song and praise characterize our response to the Lord and His work.

As hymn writer Eliza Hewitt wrote,

Singing I go along life's road,
Praising my Lord,
Praising my Lord.

Final Thought: Praise God in word and song.

A Song of Faith and Triumph

Psalm 9:10

"And they that know thy name will put their trust in thee: for thou, LORD, hast not forsaken them that seek thee."

Yesterday, we saw that God's people sing. Throughout history, God's work has inspired praise in His children. But why do they sing? God's children sing because they know God's character and His works, and they trust Him.

All praise is rooted in knowing God. The Bible often refers to God's "name" as shorthand for all that God is known to be—His attributes, His actions, His names, His glory. To know God in this way requires time invested in a personal relationship with Him, learning about Him through His Word. Then the things we learn about God provide material for our praise.

Charles Wesley reflected on God's love when he wrote, "Love Divine, All Loves Excelling." What great works of God must have inspired Isaac Watts to write "I Sing the Mighty Power of God." And think of the first time you sang "Amazing Grace" after your salvation. Each of these songs of praise is based on God's character and His work.

But intellectual knowledge alone isn't enough for genuine praise. Knowledge of God's character requires a faith-filled trust in God. Martin Luther, while facing the threat of death from both the Roman Catholic Church and the Holy Roman Empire, penned "A Mighty Fortress Is Our God" as a testimony of faith.

A more recent hymn writer, Ron Hamilton, captured the heart of faith writing,

"I could not see through the shadows ahead,
*So I looked at the cross of my Savior instead."**

These two aspects—knowing God's character and trusting Him—provide the foundation for all true Christian praise. They give us a melody to sing the songs of Zion and her King as we travel the road home.

Final Thought: What do you know about God that you can praise Him for today?

*Rejoice in the Lord, by Ron Hamilton. © 1978 by Majesty Music, Inc. All rights reserved; used by permission.

God Is Just

Psalm 10:13

"Wherefore doth the wicked condemn God? he hath said in his heart, Thou wilt not require it."

Have you noticed how the words of God's people differ from those of the ungodly? Praise characterizes those on God's path, but scorn for God typifies the wicked. Not all of the ungodly scorn God openly, but they have still scorned God by rejecting the gift of His Son. In this psalm, David observes the pride of the scornful and looks to God for judgment.

First, they relentlessly pursue their own desires (vv. 2–3). In order to have those desires, they oppress others and love what the Lord hates. They admire greedy people.

Second, they choose not to pursue God (vv. 4–6). A. W. Tozer calls the existence of God "the most fundamental reality in life," but the wicked won't give God a moment's thought. They think they are unshakeable in their ways.

Third, the wicked do not love others (vv. 7–11). Lies, cursing, strife, and emptiness characterize their speech. The wicked use other people to get what they want, and disposes of them when they're no longer needed. Displays of goodness are contrived and intended to bring glory to themselves. In spite of all this wrongdoing, the wicked arrogantly boast that God either hasn't seen them, or will not judge their sin.

But David reminds us that God sees the wicked (vv. 12–18). God responds to the humble person with tenderness, but He pours out His wrath on the unrepentant. The most carefully laid plan of the wicked will topple over like a house of cards. God breaks the stronghold of the wicked. He annihilates their schemes. Ultimately, God shows Himself as the eternal King, rejecting the wicked and upholding the humble.

Final Thought: Remember that the Lord sees the selfishness of the wicked, and He judges accordingly.

Faith Not to Flee, Part 1

Psalm 11:1

"In the LORD put I my trust: how say ye to my soul, Flee as a bird to your mountain?"

Our enemy desires to drive us off the path of God. He tempts us to look for security elsewhere and say that God is not enough. David portrays this struggle as a desire to flee from God's path into the mountains for safety. In the days of King Saul, the Israelites fled before the Philistine threat. Instead of trusting God, the people hid in caves and holes among the rocks (1 Sam. 13:5–6).

Why is it wrong to flee to the mountain? The danger is certainly real, and our enemies are intent on hurting us (v. 2). The trial or temptation you face has real teeth to it. Why shouldn't you flee?

David answers these questions in the first line of the psalm—I trust in the Lord. From this simple truth, David develops five reasons to stay in the path. Today, we'll look at the first two reasons.

First, there is no other foundation than faith in God (v. 3). If you choose to leave God's path out of fear, then where would you go? There is only one sure foundation (Luke 6:48–49; 1 Cor. 3:10–12). Leaving God's path exchanges a solid foundation for the shifting sands of the world's false security. As believers walking in God's way, we stand on the only secure footing in this storm-driven world. If we believe that God isn't sufficient, we won't find anything that is.

Second, our all-seeing God sits enthroned in heaven (v. 4). God doesn't ignore our trials, neither is He unable to intervene. Just like the Old Testament temple represented God's nearness to His people, God watches from His heavenly temple and stays with us. He watches from His throne, the symbol of unstoppable absolute power. God sees all. His evaluation of our trial is perfect and just. God sees all, and He's in complete control.

Final Thought: There is no greater place of safety than God. Put your trust in Him.

Faith Not to Flee, Part 2

Psalm 11:1

"In the LORD put I my trust: how say ye to my soul, Flee as a bird to your mountain?"

Why should we stay on the path of God when getting off seems safer? Yesterday, we saw that it's better to stay on the path because there is no place safer than God, and because God sees and controls our situation.

Let's look at three more reasons to stay on God's path during trials.

First, God lovingly tests the righteous (v. 5). Not only does God see our trials, but He also uses them to make us more like Him. We grow spiritually by persevering through trials by God's grace. Learning to trust Him in hard times increases our faith and progresses us in sanctification. God intends to draw us closer to Himself through the very trials that often entice us to seek help elsewhere. God doesn't test the wicked. He allows them to go their own way—often unhindered—to their own destruction. This is why it appears that the righteous struggle more than the wicked in this life.

Second, enemies of the righteous will face God's wrath (v. 6). The apparent advantage of the wicked is just an illusion. Any opposition—spiritual or physical—can't stand up against God. To Him, the wicked have already fallen. God has prepared a place of never-ending torment for them.

Third, we have assurance of God's unconditional love (v. 7). Nothing makes us surer in the path of God more than meditating on His unfailing love. Why would we leave the path when the King of the way loves us with everlasting love? Where could we run to find a better replacement? God smiles in love on the upright. Don't flee from His love.

Final Thought: Let nothing drive you from the path of God.

Loneliness in the Path

Psalm 12:1

"Help, LORD; for the godly man ceaseth; for the faithful fail from among the children of men."

Sometimes God leads us along lonely paths. He led Abraham out of the bustling city of Ur into the wilderness of Canaan. He led Ruth from her homeland to a place where Moabites were shunned and unwelcome. David's flight from Saul separated the young man from both family and friends. Elijah cried in the wilderness, "Lord, I've faithfully followed You, but I'm now alone." Paul often faced trouble alone when none stood with him.

Following the path of righteousness is hard, but walking it alone is even harder. The world calls more loudly when those around us join in the appeal. If only we had one companion to support us in our desire to follow hard after God! Instead, flatterers, liars, and manipulators surround us and tempt us to leave God's path. These people laugh at the way of God and at anyone who follows it.

Above the world's noise, God clearly calls to the lonely pilgrim. No matter how discouraged, the believer can find hope and joy through God's Word. Lies and flattery fall flat, but the Word of God endures forever. God speaks to lonely travelers, calling them to turn to Him for fellowship during that lonely hour. Opposed by all, faithful followers still find sweet communion with God.

Final Thought: During times of loneliness, God invites you to find fellowship with Him.

Singing When God Delays

Psalm 13:1

"How long wilt thou forget me, O LORD? for ever? how long wilt thou hide thy face from me?"

No one enjoys being forgotten. Consider how it feels when a friend—or worse, a loved one—forgets your birthday. Or think how you feel when someone you've gone to meet never shows up for the appointment. We'd probably all agree that being forgotten hurts.

When it seems like God has forgotten us, we often respond with worry, fear, and frustration. Perhaps you've prayed for grace during a painful illness, but instead of improving, you feel worse each day. Maybe you've asked for wisdom and guidance in making a decision, but when the deadline arrives, you're still unsure. Or you've earnestly begged God to heal a broken relationship, but the breach only widens. Experiencing a similar trial and feeling forgotten, David cried out, "How long, O Lord?"

How do we respond when God appears to delay? What can we do when we feel lost and alone? David reminds us of the right response: to reflect on God's character and rejoice in Him.

When God delays, remember what you know about Him. How can we doubt His merciful love when we meditate on His gift of salvation? We are told and shown repeatedly that His mercy and abiding love never end. Reflect on the ways God has shown that mercy and love throughout a lifetime, rather than focusing on the snapshot of this one moment.

As we reflect on God's character, we can't help praising and thanking Him. Rejoice in God's bountiful love and faithful provision, as David did (vv. 5–6). Sing of your God and of the hope He gives. Remember your heavenly Father, for He certainly remembers you.

Final Thought: When God delays, remember His goodness and praise Him.

We've All Walked the Wrong Path

Psalm 14:3

"They are all gone aside, they are all together become filthy: there is none that doeth good, no, not one."

When we contrast God's path with the path of the wicked, it's easy to take pride in choosing the right way. We may be tempted to think, "I'm pretty great. I walk God's path while much of the world happily follows the path of the wicked." The Pharisees in Jesus' day had a similar response, and nobody wants to keep that kind of company!

The Bible clearly teaches that no person—besides Christ—ever perfectly followed God's path. Every one of us has sinned and fallen short of God's standard (Rom. 3:23). Not only have we corrupted ourselves, but we've also contributed to the corruption of others. God's evaluation, as He searches for those who seek Him, is echoed in Psalm 14:3—no one does good.

The truth of our depravity should humble us before our God, and remind us of our need for His mercy and grace. We lament with Paul (Rom. 7:24), Peter (Luke 5:8), Isaiah (Isa. 6:5) and others, "Oh wretched man that I am! Who can save me?" If we follow the way of righteousness, we certainly don't deserve credit. Our Savior rescued us, and all the credit belongs to Him.

How did our Savior move us from our natural, sinful path to God's way? Isaiah 53:6 provides the answer. The verse first acknowledges the problem—"all we like sheep have gone astray." Then, it shows God's solution. He took all of our sin and placed it on the crucified Christ, who took our punishment. Through this gift of salvation, God moves us from the broad way, which ends in destruction, to the narrow way, which continues into everlasting life.

Final Thought: Thank God for putting you on the path of life.

The Characteristics of God's Worshippers, Part 1

Psalm 15:1

"Lord, who shall abide in thy tabernacle? who shall dwell in thy holy hill?"

In David's time, the Israelites worshipped God at the Tabernacle—a beautiful tent-like structure constructed during Israel's wilderness wanderings. The mobility of the tent portrayed God's faithful presence with Israel as the people journeyed to the Promised Land. This way, God ensured that His people had the opportunity to continually dwell in His presence. For believers, God now maintains His constant presence in our lives through the Holy Spirit.

Not only does God grant us continual access to Him, but He also develops certain characteristics in those who continually worship Him. In this psalm, David lists several of these qualities and categorizes them in two ways: loving God and loving others.

All true spiritual change must begin with love for God. Without a foundational love for God, our outward spirituality is hypocrisy. Paul compares our loveless deeds—even good ones—to blaring trumpets and crashing cymbals (1 Cor. 13:1). We may get a lot of attention, but we're just producing a lot of meaningless noise. For the believer, an honest evaluation of the heart (Ps. 15:2) will reveal the motivation behind outward behavior. If we simply love impressing others, we know our righteous acts are self-righteousness, despised by God. But if we find a true, love-inspired faith in God at our core, then we'll reflect God's righteousness to others.

Final Thought: True abiding worship begins in your heart.

The Characteristics of God's Worshippers, Part 2

Psalm 15:5b

"He that doeth these things shall never be moved."

Yesterday, we saw that God gives us constant access to His presence, and that He produces certain qualities in believers who dwell there. Believers who fellowship with God will develop a foundational love for Him. That love for God impacts relationships with other people.

The words of those who abide with God (v. 3)

We all know the childhood rhyme "Sticks and stones may break my bones, but words will never hurt me" is a complete falsehood. Words do hurt. But when we dwell in God's presence and worship Him, our words change from hurtful to helpful. Our conversation consists of praising God and encouraging others, instead of tearing others apart. If we hear "dirt" on someone, we don't pay attention to it or repeat it to someone else. God changes our tongue, that "unruly evil" (James 3:6), into a beneficial tool.

The wisdom of those who abide with God (v. 4a)

Not only does God change our speech when we abide in Him, but He also gives us wisdom to make right choices. Walking with God allows us to discern and judge good and evil correctly (Heb. 5:14). We can identify evil as evil, and good as good. That may seem simple to do, but unbelievers don't have this ability.

The actions of those who abide with God (vv. 4b–5)

Fellowship with God affects our actions, as well as our words. We keep our promises—even when it's difficult to do so—because we abide in a faithful God. We give to those in need and expect nothing in return (Luke 6:35). And we'd never allow potential personal benefits—like people's praise or bribes—to influence our choices between right and wrong. In our relationships, we act toward others the way God acts toward us.

And what is the expectation of those who dwell with God in this way? If we continually stay in God's presence, we will never be moved from God's path.

Final Thought: Let your fellowship with God overflow into your relationships with people.

The Pleasure of God's Path

Psalm 16:11

"Thou wilt shew me the path of life: in thy presence is fulness of joy; at thy right hand there are pleasures for evermore."

Have you noticed how much we crave pleasure? Yet so much of this world's pleasure leaves us unfulfilled. God created in us the capability to enjoy Him and find true pleasure in Him alone. He is the only source of fulfillment and joy, from which all good things flow (James 1:17).

In Psalm 16, David expresses his trust in the Lord (vv. 1–2a). A Christian will experience delight in a humble, intimate relationship with God. David mentions four specific pleasures that Christians enjoy on God's path.

We find pleasure in the company of our fellow travelers, the saints (v. 3). When we gather with other believers, we find refreshment, encouragement, and accountability. We enjoy our unity as we worship God together.

We find joy in our inheritance in Christ (vv. 4–5). We will receive glory and heaven's riches at our journey's end, but we don't have to wait for heaven to experience all of God's gifts. God ministers to us right now through His relationship with us and our relationships with other believers.

We experience joy in the counsel of His Word (vv. 6–7). He guides us by both precept and example. As we set Christ's life and ministry before us, we have joy in following in His footsteps.

Finally, we rejoice in the promise of security in Christ (vv. 9–10). No one can remove us from God's protective hand (John 10:28) or take away our salvation. In Christ, we are secure forever.

Final Thought: Follow after God and allow Him to shower you with lasting pleasures that only He can provide.

The Apple of God's Eye

Psalm 17:8

"Keep me as the apple of the eye, hide me under the shadow of thy wings."

The Bible contains many word pictures showing God's care for His children. God acts as a Good Shepherd over His sheep. He stands like a tower of refuge and safety for His people. The Father-child analogy portrays God's tender love and care. But none of these pictures conveys the level of intimacy like God keeping us as the "apple of His eye."

The "apple of the eye" refers to the pupil—the opening at the center of the eye which admits light and allows us to see. Though this opening is small, it's guarded by many levels of protection. The pupil is surrounded by the iris, which dilates or contracts to manage the amount of light entering the eye. The iris is supported by the strong and durable sclera—the white of the eye. The lens—a transparent dome—covers the layers beneath it. In turn, the eyelids and lashes guard the lens and defend against larger debris. Finally, tiny ducts at the corner of the eye lubricate the whole system with tears.

In addition to testifying of God's creative power, the intricate protection of the eye creates a wonderful picture of God's care and protection for us. God keeps us with the same excessive protection that our pupils receive. Though our eyes will eventually fail us, God's protection will never fail.

Final Thought: You are the apple of God's eye.

The Power of God's Protection

Psalm 18:3

"I will call upon the LORD, who is worthy to be praised: so shall I be saved from mine enemies."

Watching someone we love go through a trial is agony. This is especially true when we are powerless to help him or her in the trial. Care without power to intervene reveals the frailty of human ability, but God knows no such limits.

Psalm 17 portrayed the intimacy of God's care for His people, and Psalm 18 expounds on the incredible power of that care. This power of God inspires love (v. 1), praise (vv. 3, 49) and faith (v. 48). David's praise climaxes in verse 46 as he proclaims, "The Lord liveth; and blessed be my rock; and let the God of my salvation be exalted." Let's take a moment to look at this amazing power.

David illustrates God's power in battle. God is the strong fortress standing against the enemy, the shield that no missiles can pierce (v. 2). He is the horn announcing our salvation (v. 2). His arrows scatter the enemy (v. 14), and nothing can save the wicked from His wrath (v. 41).

But God is far more powerful than implements of war. When God moves against the enemy, the earth shakes before Him (v. 7). Fire pours down on the enemies of God's people (v. 8) and the winds of heaven beat them (v. 10). God causes even the earth to fight against the wicked.

Yet God, who possesses unequal power, still cares for His own. He pulls them out of the floods of the battle (v. 16). He snatches them from the enemy's hand (v. 17) and puts His children in the place of blessing (vv. 19–20). Ultimately, He sets up the righteous to rule over the wicked (vv. 43–44). This God is our God.

Final Thought: God, in His great power, will triumph for His glory in your life.

You Can't Miss It

Psalm 19:4

"Their line is gone out through all the earth, and their words to the end of the world. In them hath he set a tabernacle for the sun."

In 1931, a man named Ted Hustead purchased the only drug store in the small town of Wall, South Dakota. Normally the store's business would have suffered in such a remote location, but thanks to the opening of Mt. Rushmore and creative advertising, Hustead transformed the tiny drug store into one of the largest attractions in the area. Wall Drug placed signs all over South Dakota and neighboring states offering free water to thirsty travelers. As the drugstore became a sensation, its signs advanced across the United States and the world. Thanks to widespread advertising along highways, now Wall Drug is hard to miss.

In Psalm 19, David states that the heavens declare God's glory (v. 1). Day and night, all creation points to the Creator (v. 2). In fact, no place exists where the glory of God is not on constant display. All of creation is His billboard.

These divine billboards line the paths of the righteous and the wicked. The wicked try to ignore or deny God's glory and focus instead on life's empty pleasures. But even though the wicked refuse to give due honor to God, nature never ceases its song of praise. You just can't miss it.

Final Thought: God clearly displays His glory, even to those who refuse to see it.

Sustained by His Name

Psalm 20:7

"Some trust in chariots, and some in horses: but we will remember the name of the LORD our God."

In David's day, horses and chariots provided a significant advantage in warfare. Swift and agile, a chariot made a difficult target for the enemy to hit. It allowed for ranged or melee attacks from its occupants, and the chariot itself could be used as a weapon to cut down infantry.

Even though horses and chariots possessed such strength, speed, and mobility, David chose to trust the name of the Lord instead of such a powerful weapon. Why? Because God is stronger than any weapon, and He personally cares for His children. When we trust God in times of trouble, He consistently responds in four ways.

- God sends help and support (v. 2).
- God remembers worship (v. 3).
- God grants petitions (vv. 4–5).
- God saves (v. 6).

As if such promises were not enough to claim our trust, David gives another reason to place faith in God. He contrasts the outcome of the two types of faith. Those who trust in weapons and powers of this world will "collapse and fall," but those who look to God will "rise and stand" (v. 8). We are sustained by His name.

Final Thought: Weigh carefully where you place your faith.

When God Seems Distant

Psalm 22:1

"My God, my God, why hast thou forsaken me? why art thou so far from helping me, and from the words of my roaring?"

The darkest moments along the path of God are those when we feel God has forsaken us. All of God's children experience these moments, and David was no exception. Throughout Scripture we see many saints feeling abandoned—the Israelites enslaved in Egypt, Elijah fleeing from Jezebel, and Habakkuk upon his watchtower.

Christ experienced poignant separation, evidenced in the words He spoke from the cross. Deserted by His disciples, rejected by His people, and condemned by the government, He hung alone and forsaken. He felt the ultimate pain when He carried the sin of the world, and God turned away from Him. This separation between God and God had never before existed. Such separation seemed impossible. In response, the sky darkened at midday and the earth shook. The darkness lasted only three hours, but no other hours in all history held such divine terror.

That period of terror and darkness ultimately brought great joy. All the rejection we deserved was poured out on Christ. Our sins separated Him from the Father, but His sacrifice guarantees that they will no longer separate us from God.

The Father will never leave us nor forsake us (Heb. 13:5). Sin may harm our fellowship, but because of the cross, it can never separate our souls from God.

Final Thought: Rest today in the assurance of God's continual, loving presence.

Led by the Good Shepherd, Part 1

Psalm 23:3

"He restoreth my soul: he leadeth me in the paths of righteousness for his name's sake."

This much-loved psalm shows how God lovingly leads and cares for His people. Not only has God revealed our path, but He has also committed to guide and sustain us on our journey. Because many dangers and difficulties lie in our path, we must have a Shepherd to lead us.

The first promise we find in this psalm is for provision (v. 1). God knows our needs better than we know them. He withholds nothing good or necessary from His flock. Such knowledge grants us peace and confidence as we travel our path with God.

Following close behind the promise of provision, we find the promise of rest. The Shepherd knows that His sheep need fresh grass and calm waters to find nourishment and refreshment. The scrub grasses of the desert may serve in a pinch, but the sheep cannot survive long on such a diet. Our good Shepherd knows our needs as well, and He ordains times of peace and refreshment. You may be in the desert at the moment, but God is preparing your next place of rest so He can restore your soul.

Final Thought: The Lord is your Shepherd, and He provides for you.

Led by the Good Shepherd, Part 2

Psalm 23:3

"He restoreth my soul: he leadeth me in the paths of righteousness for his name's sake."

Previously, in Psalm 23, we saw that God provides for our needs and gives us rest. But far more important than provision and rest is the promise of guidance in righteousness. Without this guidance, we will naturally follow the path of sin and wickedness—the path ending in destruction. There is no righteousness in us, so we need Christ's righteousness. As God ascribes righteousness to the life of a fallen sinner, He receives glory for a task impossible by human standards.

The promises in verse 4 emphasize that every path through this sin-blighted world will include dark valleys. The troubles and suffering of these times are real, but the promise of our Shepherd's presence is real, as well. He uses His rod and staff to guide us through these dark places and to remind us of His presence, so that we have no need to fear.

The final promise in verse 5 assures us of abundant provision, even in the face of opposition. Do enemies trouble you on the path? God rebukes them by giving you a feast in their presence. He pours out His anointing on you and fills your cup to overflow with blessings.

With such a Shepherd we can walk the path with confidence. In this life, He will surround us with His divine goodness and loving mercies. And after this life, He has prepared us an eternal home in His presence.

Final Thought: The Lord is my Shepherd, and He guides me.

Standing on God's Holy Hill

Psalm 24:3

"Who shall ascend into the hill of the LORD? or who shall stand in his holy place?"

The most holy place in the Old Testament was Mount Moriah. On this hill Abraham bound Isaac and prepared to offer him to the Lord. On this same site, David set up the tabernacle with the recovered Ark of the Covenant, and later, Solomon built the first Jewish temple. But the most important event occurred when God Himself sanctified this hill with His presence.

No sensible person would ascend the hill without considering its significance. Certainly no one would enter the temple without preparing his heart and bringing a sacrifice. To come into God's presence required cleansing from the dirt and sin of daily living.

Even today, we need preparation to enter God's presence. Through Christ we have everyday access, and the Spirit sanctifies us in preparation for our eternal abode in God's presence. He is working to cleanse our hands and our hearts of all the vanity and falsehood drawing us away from God (v. 4). He ministers to us the blessing of the Lord and the righteousness of Christ (v. 5). He works that we might seek after our God.

Final Thought: Our path culminates in the presence of God.

Teach Me Your Paths

Psalm 25:4

"Shew me thy ways, O LORD; teach me thy paths."

The heart of every Christian should echo the prayer of David in this psalm. Sometimes as we walk God's path, it's a struggle to know the way He would have us to go. We face many forks in the road and, at times, apparently dead ends. When faced with these choices, our own wisdom fails. We need a Teacher.

Moses felt his heavy need for guidance as the people of Israel prepared to leave Mt. Sinai (see Exo. 33). The way to Sinai had been hard enough—filled with complaints, hunger, thirst, and enemy attacks. Arriving at Sinai, the people proved even more stubborn and prone to disobedience. Finally, God called Moses back into the wilderness with its unfamiliar paths and unknown dangers. Moses expressed concern. He prayed, "Lord, show me your ways" (v. 13). He requested more than mere directions. He desired to know God intimately and experience God's grace.

Today, we have the same need. The way ahead may not be a literal wilderness, but it is unknown. We need God to teach us His ways and His paths. We must know both how to walk and where to walk. As we desire to be led in His truth, let this be the prayer of every heart that seeks Him.

Final Thought: Ask the Lord to reveal Himself and His way to you today.

What the Lord Remembers

Psalm 25:7

"Remember not the sins of my youth, nor my transgressions: according to thy mercy remember thou me for thy goodness' sake, O LORD."

David's request in the first part of this psalm—"Lord, teach me your paths"—clashes with David's sin. His sin is an affront to a righteous God, and so it would seem that David has no hope for God's assistance. However, David asks God in faith not to "remember" his sins.

We use the word remember to mean recalling information—such as remembering a name. But that's not the type of remembering this verse indicates. God remembers all things because He is all-knowing, or omniscient. In Scripture, the word remember means to act upon known information. David prays, in essence, "Lord, You know all my sins, but I am asking you not to respond to me in the way my sin deserves."

How could David ask God not to act on his offensive sin? He could pray this way because he had come to God in an attitude of faith and humility, seeking forgiveness. God's character assures that forgiveness. God is merciful and loving (v. 6), as well as good and upright (v. 8a). The dilemma of God's goodness and justice is solved perfectly through Christ's sacrifice. He offers forgiveness of our sins through the payment of Christ, guiding us to salvation (v. 8b).

What is our response to such grace? First, we approach God with meekness and humility (v. 9). We deserve nothing and demand nothing, but we receive all God gives us with thanksgiving and submission. Second, we respond with reverence and fear (vv. 12, 14). Knowing that God hates sin and judges disobedience, we respond with obedience to His word. God's great love and mercy should inspire such a response in all believers.

Final Thought: God remembers your sins no more.

People Worth Avoiding

Psalm 26:5

"I have hated the congregation of evil doers; and will not sit with the wicked."

The Christian life is a team sport. God uses the people we fellowship with to sharpen us spiritually and encourage us in the path of righteousness. David stated that he loved spending time in God's house (v. 8) and with God's people (v. 12).

But not all people encourage us in our walk with the Lord. David mentions four types of people that we must avoid making our close friends (vv. 4–5).

- The vain person—This person loves falsehood and shallow living and can talk for hours without saying anything of spiritual value.

- The hypocrite—This person can put on a religious front when needed but quickly changes when the situation demands it.

- The evildoer—This person is known for causing problems and stirring up trouble.

- The wicked—This person has a reputation for questionable morals.

The passage does not command us to avoid all contact with such people. We should share with them God's glory and His offer of salvation. But we must avoid making them our constant companions, because it's likely they will harm our walk, not help it.

Final Thought: Make close friends of those who love God.

No Fear

Psalm 27:1

"The LORD is my light and my salvation; whom shall I fear? the LORD is the strength of my life; of whom shall I be afraid?"

For most of us, it's hard to imagine life without fear. Yet fear wasn't a part of God's intent for humankind—it didn't exist in Eden. Adam and Eve never feared losing a job, getting cancer, or running out of money. Fear only entered that perfect world through sin.

Sin brought death and separation. As people recognize their limitations and fail to trust God, they grow afraid. Anger, greed, and envy separate relationships. The reality of death confronts us daily through sickness, murder, injuries, and even aging.

How can we experience peace when life offers none? We can trust the God of peace who ultimately saves us from sin's consequences. We can confidently repeat David's words, "The Lord is my light and my salvation; the Lord is my strength and life."

Here humankind's four greatest fears are answered.

- I don't have the knowledge or wisdom I need—the Lord is my light.
- I fear the consequences of my sin—the Lord is my salvation.
- I am too weak to face the challenges of life—the Lord is my strength.
- I fear illness and death—the Lord is my life.

Because the all-powerful God holds us in hands of love, we have no need to fear.

Final Thought: God's love and grace answer all your fears.

Finding Courage

Psalm 27:14

"Wait on the LORD: be of good courage, and he shall strengthen thine heart: wait, I say, on the LORD."

As we saw previously, we have no cause for fear when we trust God. But how exactly do we find courage in God? Like Peter walking on the water, our eyes of faith easily turn from Christ to the battering winds and waves threatening to snuff out our life. When we take our eyes off Jesus, we instead focus on our fears. How then do we keep gazing on Christ when so many fears demand our attention?

The story of Peter's amazing walk of faith gives us the secret to conquer fear. We often emphasize Peter's lack of faith which caused him to sink into the waves, and by doing so we forget an amazing part of the story. Peter walked on water. It wasn't James, John, or any of the others—they waited in the boat. Peter saw Christ and found the courage to do the impossible. Peter's fears returned only when he stopped focusing on Christ.

Just as Peter needed to gaze only on Christ, so we should keep our focus on Him. David speaks of that same need in this psalm. In the face of fearful circumstances (vv. 2–3), David states that his one desire is to gaze upon the beauty of the Lord (v. 4). He responds to God's invitation to see His face (v. 8). David turned his eyes to God.

And what was the result? David found confident strength in God's goodness (v. 13). Finally, David instructs his listeners to wait upon the Lord to find courage and strength in Him.

Final Thought: Fear can only possess your heart when you fail to gaze upon the Lord.

Two Expectations

Psalm 28:7

"The LORD is my strength and my shield; my heart trusted in him, and I am helped: therefore my heart greatly rejoiceth; and with my song will I praise him."

Are you a person of prayer? Prayer evidences faith in the fact that God deals differently with those who seek Him and those who do not. If God were silent, then the righteous would have no different end than the wicked (v. 1b). But in our trials, we believe God hears and answers with mercy and power (v. 2). There is a very different expectation for those who live life without God and those who call to Him in faith.

David speaks of the differing expectations of the works of the wicked and the faith of the righteous. He asks God to differentiate clearly between the outcomes of both approaches to life. He prays that God would give the wicked their earnings. The wicked will receive the reward of their works (v. 4). Because they rejected the Lord and His works, God will tear them down.

The righteous are different (v. 7). They trust in God, not their own labor. They find help from their Lord. They rejoice and sing of His works and not their own. Instead of the expectation of destruction, they find the salvation, care, and provision of the Good Shepherd.

Final Thought: Rejoicing comes from faith in God, not from laboring in your own strength.

The Glory Due Our Mighty King

Psalm 29:1

"Give unto the LORD, O ye mighty, give unto the LORD glory and strength."

David addresses this psalm to "the mighty." The word he uses is the Hebrew word ben'el, meaning "sons of the mighty" or "sons of the Almighty." He tells the strong and powerful to give glory and honor to the Lord, the eternal King (v. 10). Compared to the strength of the Lord, the power of humankind is nothing.

David doesn't focus on the might of God's arm or on God's amazing deeds. Instead, he points to the power of God's voice. What can the Lord do with only a word?

- His voice thunders like a mighty storm (vv. 3–4).
- His voice breaks up the cedars of Lebanon—the strongest trees in ancient Israel (vv. 5–6).
- His voice shoots lightning and flame (v. 7).
- His voice shakes the wilderness with earthquakes (v. 8).
- His voice makes the deer give birth (v. 9).
- His voice levels forests (v. 9).

David records the only appropriate response to such power—we should worship and glorify God for His strength, and for the strength He bestows on us through His love.

Final Thought: Glorify God with the strength He gives you.

Temporary Sorrow, Eternal Joy

Psalm 30:5

"For his anger endureth but a moment; in his favour is life: weeping may endure for a night, but joy cometh in the morning."

Just as every rose has its thorns, every journey along God's path has both pleasant and painful moments. Here, David offers an encouraging reminder for hard times—on God's path, sorrow and suffering have limits. The Lord draws up His saints out of their troubles (v. 1).

When a Christian sins, what hope does he or she have? Sin causes broken fellowship, hurt, and ultimately, God's correction. When we sin, we deserve the Lord's just anger. But because of Christ's payment, the Lord's anger rested on the Son, not on us. When we confess our sin, He forgives us completely (1 John 1:9) and restores His favor—the blessing of the redeemed—to us.

How can we hope in the midst of grief? In addition to the sorrows of our sin, we experience the pain that accompanies a sin-cursed world—sickness, loss, and death. For the Christian, these hurts are only temporary. God answers prayer and gives grace, replacing sorrow with peace and joy. Though pain may endure our entire lives, God will wipe away every tear at the dawn of eternity (Rev. 21:4).

Final Thought: Take courage. God gives joy and hope to the sorrowing saint.

Deliver Me from Snares

Psalm 31:3

"For thou art my rock and my fortress; therefore for thy name's sake lead me, and guide me."

If you ever travel through the hills east of the Sea of Galilee, you'll see many red, triangular signs along the road, reading, "Danger, landmine area." Suddenly, you become very aware of the dangers near your path and those green fields appear much less inviting.

Our spiritual walk with God traverses areas of danger as well—external attacks, as well as those from our own flesh. Some dangers are easy to spot and avoid, but others are subtle and can trap even the wary traveler. In the middle of such opposition, how can we hope to emerge unhurt?

God alone is our firm rock and safe fortress, protecting and delivering us. He guides His saints on their journey, directing glory to His name. When we get tangled in a trap, He pulls us from the enemy's nets. Just as we trusted Christ to redeem us from our sins, so we can confidently commit our ways completely into His hands.

Final Thought: God is the only true refuge. Trust your ways to Him.

Recognizing the Snares

Psalm 31:16

"Make thy face to shine upon thy servant: save me for thy mercies' sake."

What snares do we encounter on our path in this life? While temptation takes many forms, David narrows them down to three general categories in this psalm.

First, the world's gods can lure us away from our path (v. 6). Every day, we encounter the temptation to pursue the temporal pleasures around us. The world offers us the desires of our flesh and eyes, and all it asks in return is our love and worship (1 John 2:15–17). God warns that all these things pass away.

Second, we face temptations from our own sin nature (v. 9). The pull of our flesh is real and strong. Though it promises satisfaction, it slowly saps us of life and joy. Instead of finding satisfaction, we get only weakness and sorrow.

Third, adversaries try to drive us off the path (vv. 11–13). They mock and reject our choice to follow God's path, and they will even try to hurt us. But remember that no persecution can compare to the joy that awaits us at the end of our journey, and God surrounds us with His power.

In the face of such opposition, our only hope is to trust the Lord and place our lives in His hands (v. 24). As we live by faith, we find His salvation, mercy, and love. We can safely hope in the Lord (v. 24).

Final Thought: As His child, the Lord will preserve you from snares along the way.

The Song of Forgiveness

Psalm 32:1

"Blessed is he whose transgression is forgiven, whose sin is covered."

Ever since Adam and Eve were expelled from the Garden of Eden, humankind has dealt with the pain of sin's consequences. Before salvation, our sin condemns us, and after salvation, our sin grieves our righteous God and breaks our fellowship with Him. The longer we live the Christian life, the more troubled we are at seeing the effect of sin on our lives.

How can we rejoice when burdened by so great a curse? How can our groaning (vv. 3–4) change to singing?

The answer comes from an unlikely Person—the One against whom we sin. In love, God covers us with His mercy and asks only for our confession and repentance (v. 5). He freely grants forgiveness. We sing because of the loving reconciliation Christ provided by His death. We no longer wait for justly deserved condemnation. Instead, the Lord surrounds us with His mercy (v. 10).

Final Thought: Let God's mercy inspire a song of joy and forgiveness in you.

Let the Righteous Rejoice

Psalm 33:1

"Rejoice in the LORD, O ye righteous: for praise is comely for the upright."

As a child of God, you enjoy the covering of Christ's righteousness. The nakedness of Eden vanishes under the white robes of your Savior. So clothed, you can stand once more before the God of the universe, not as a condemned sinner, but as a beloved son. Meditate on this great truth. Let it sink into your heart.

Does this truth touch something inside you? Does it stir some deep song of praise?

Praise is the heart cry of the redeemed. Some break forth in song. Others find their pen loosed in words of praise. For David, praise flowed through his shepherd harp. Whatever creativity God has given you, He intended it as a tool to declare His praise.

And how should we praise Him? Verse three tells us. We praise Him skillfully, developing the talents we have to better reflect His glory. Even more, we praise Him loudly. No shame of our Father. No reserve in declaring His infinite glory. The world cannot ignore the loud praise of God's saints.

Final Thought: Today, let praise ring forth loudly from your life.

The Cause of Our Praise

Psalm 33:18

"Behold, the eye of the LORD is upon them that fear him, upon them that hope in his mercy."

Our salvation in Christ is reason enough to inspire praise. However, David offers three other truths about God to ignite our worship.

God's words and actions are right and powerful (vv. 6–9).

When God speaks, nothing can prevent His will. He spoke, and the universe appeared out of nothing. At His command, the oceans gathered together and were held in place. Such incredible power of a loving God gives us confidence in His rule. Praise Him for His power.

God loves righteousness and justice (vv. 10–17).

The plans of the ungodly fail, but God's plan stands firm. The wicked gathers armies and war machines, but their attempts to resist the will of God are futile. God rules in omnipotence from His throne and does His will regardless. Praise Him for His righteous rule.

God shows eternal goodness to His people (vv. 18–22).

God is good. He shows loyal love to those who place their hope in Him. He provides strength and security for His children. His mercy answers our faith. What can we do but praise Him for His goodness?

Final Thought: Reflect on the character and word of God, and let that knowledge fuel your praise.

Learn the Fear of the Lord, Part 1

Psalm 34:9

"O fear the LORD, ye his saints: for there is no want to them that fear him."

Solomon concluded the Book of Ecclesiastes with the two-fold duty of humankind—fear God and keep His commandments. We readily understand the concept of keeping commandments because we live in a world full of rules and laws. But it's more difficult for us to understand the concept of fearing God. How can we fear a God we love?

There are at least two kinds of fear—positive and negative. Our fallen world focuses on a negative, sin-created fear, such as dread of potential danger. I may lose my job; I might get cancer; something might be living under my bed. In fact, some studies show that 95% of the things we fear never come to pass. God commands us to cast our cares on Him, so that we don't need to be anxious for the future.

Fearing the Lord in this way reveals a wrong view of God. Some view God as a tyrannical deity just waiting to strike them down with lightning should they step out of line.

To fear the Lord is to have a reverent respect, awe, and worship for the sovereign, omnipotent Lord of all things. It's the kind of healthy respect we would show to a good boss or a good king—but, unlike human authorities, God fully deserves our highest worship. At its heart, fear knows God for who He is and responds in reverence.

Final Thought: Fear and revere God for His character.

Learn the Fear of the Lord, Part 2

Psalm 34:11

"Come, ye children, hearken unto me: I will teach you the fear of the LORD."

We saw yesterday that the fear of the Lord differs from worldly fears. Sinful fear tries to imprison us in anxiety and helplessness, but the fear of the Lord produces reverence for God. What does reverence look like? David lists three areas where the fear of the Lord manifests itself.

In our words (v. 13)

God speaks words of comfort, truth, and justice. His words formed worlds, condemned sin, and promised salvation. If we fear Him, we will align our speech with His. When we reflect God's character in our speech, we will despise sinful words and lies.

In our actions (v. 14a)

The fear of God motivates and enables us to reflect God's glory in our actions. Our relationship with a holy God changes our fleshly desires into righteous ones. Instead of pleasing ourselves, we will do good to others as God has done good to us.

In our pursuits (v. 14b)

God is the God of all peace. As we reverence Him, we desire to be instruments of His peace. We share the message of peace with the lost. We proclaim the peace of repentance to those overtaken by sin. As Paul admonishes in Romans 14:19, we pursue the things which promote peace and edify, or build up, one another.

Final Thought: Let your fear of the Lord motivate your words, actions, and pursuits.

Delivered Out of Troubles

Psalm 34:19

"Many are the afflictions of the righteous: but the LORD delivereth him out of them all."

How do we respond to the fears and troubles in this world? While much of what we worry over never comes to pass, we do face real problems. What does Psalm 34 tell us about these?

David talks about both fear and troubles. First, he addresses the world's fears. Verse 4 tells us that as we pursue God, He delivers us from those things we fear. The more we know about our Father, the less room we have to fear. The Spirit within us is not a Spirit of fear but of power, love, and a sound mind. (2 Tim. 1:7). Fear that worries over "what if?" is always a product of our flesh, not of the Spirit.

Troubles, on the other hand, are very real and common problems that we face (v. 19). While God promises to deliver us from fear, He does not make such a promise about troubles and afflictions. In this psalm, God promises three times to deliver us, not "from" troubles but "out of" them. The difference is striking. In our fallen world, we experience distress. But as followers of Christ, we are assured that every valley on our path has a purpose, and that God will bring us out of each valley at the right moment. We may see His deliverance in this life, or we may not see it until death—when all valleys cease for the righteous. The wicked perish in adversity, but God protects the righteous when they face affliction because they are no longer condemned (v. 22).

Final Thought: Do not fear. Trust God in all your troubles.

The Lord, Our Champion

Psalm 35:1

"Plead my cause, O LORD, with them that strive with me: fight against them that fight against me."

Our modern usage of the word champion typically reminds us of sports. The champions are the people who win the most recent Super Bowl or World Cup. But this is a very recent usage of the word. Traditionally, a champion is a representative who fights for a cause, or fights in the place of another.

David knew the meaning of a champion. He had faced the Philistine champion, Goliath. David himself served as a champion in Saul's army, "slaying his ten thousands" (1 Sam. 18:7). Yet David knew that he needed a greater Champion who could fight against his enemies.

David pursued God's glory, and He knew that God would fight for him in his cause. He envisions God arrayed in armor with His spear drawn against the wicked. David sits securely as the Champion of champions fights on his behalf.

In our pursuit of God's way and God's glory, we too will face opposition. What a comfort to know that God fights for us. He will not keep silent. He is our salvation.

Final Thought: Be of good cheer. The Lord fights for those who pursue His ways.

Love Your Enemies

Psalm 35:14

"I behaved myself as though he had been my friend or brother: I bowed down heavily, as one that mourneth for his mother."

During his prayer for God to take vengeance on his enemies, David inserts an important interlude. In verses 13 and 14, he reveals that he had treated these people with family-like love. In their times of sorrow, David had treated them like friends, brothers, even as he would his own mother. Yet they responded to his kindness by treating him wrongfully, repaying evil for good.

This reminds us of an important truth. Even though people may be the immediate instruments of our affliction, something much deeper factors into their behavior. A sinful, depraved nature lies at the heart of every enemy's attack. In fact, this sin affects our enemies as much as it affects us—perhaps more so. We experience pain and defamation, but our attackers harbor sin in their hearts, separating themselves from God.

Jesus instructs us to love our enemies and to do good to those who wrong us (Matt. 5:43–48). By doing so, we reflect our heavenly Father who loved us when we were still His enemies. We show the impartiality of a God who sends His rain on the just and the unjust.

Final Thought: Ask God for the grace to truly love and care for your enemies.

The Excellency of God's Steadfast Love

Psalm 36:5

"Thy mercy, O LORD, is in the heavens; and thy faithfulness reacheth unto the clouds."

The Hebrew word for the highest form of love is hesed. It indicates a steadfast love that unconditionally shows mercy and kindness to the object of that love. The vast majority of passages that use this word use it in reference to God showing His steadfast love.

Psalm 36 contains three stanzas that praise God's steadfast love.

God's steadfast love is immense (vv. 5–6). David lists four pillars of God's character—love, faithfulness, righteousness, and justice. He compares them to the height of the heavens, the greatness of mountains, and the depths of the deepest sea.

God's steadfast love is the place of blessing (vv. 7–9). We enjoy the blessings of comfort and rest under God's wings. He invites us to feast at His banqueting table and drink out of the rivers of His pleasure. In His light, we see light.

God's steadfast love is a continuing blessing to His people (vv. 10–12). God gives good things to both the righteous and the wicked, such as food, beauty, and sunshine, but for the righteous such blessings never end. They grow in this life and bloom bright and eternal in the life to come.

Final Thought: Praise the Lord for the greatness of His steadfast love.

Two Responses to God's Steadfast Love

Psalm 36:7

"How excellent is thy lovingkindness, O God! therefore the children of men put their trust under the shadow of thy wings."

All people enjoy a measure of God's love and goodness. God sends sun and rain upon both the just and the unjust (Matt. 5:45). The unsaved and the saint can both appreciate the beauty of a sunset or savor the tanginess of a grapefruit. But the saved and unsaved differ in their response to such gifts.

The psalm begins with the wicked person's response to God's goodness. The wicked selfishly accepts God's good blessings but doesn't allow them to change the heart. The wicked person breaks God's laws and lives as he or she pleases. This person continually tells lies and plans evil. He or she simply misses, or ignores, the message of God's general blessings.

The righteous person views God's love and responds with trust and submission. A God who creates a good world out of infinite resources is the only One who can truly satisfy. His faithful character is reflected by the constant laws of nature. The abundant resources of our world direct our focus to the Giver of every good and perfect gift.

Final Thought: How have you responded to God's blessings in the past week?

Alternatives to Fretting

Psalm 37:7

"Rest in the LORD, and wait patiently for him: fret not thyself because of him who prospereth in his way, because of the man who bringeth wicked devices to pass."

How often do we feel frustration when we see the easy success of the wicked? Why does their way get to be broad, smooth, and pleasant? Thinking about such things without a proper view of God can lead to envy, anger, and even temptation. The Bible calls this train of thought "fretting," and David warns against it three separate times (vv. 1, 7, 8).

Instead of fretful anger over the wicked, David offers a five-part alternative that focuses on God.

- Trust the Lord and do good (v. 3). Realizing that God is in control, leave the details to Him and continue to live with love for God and others.

- Delight in the Lord (v. 4). Recognize that you have the true source of joy that the wicked can never know.

- Commit your way to the Lord (v. 5). Entrust your path to your loving Father, knowing He has good planned for you.

- Rest in the Lord (v. 7). Wait patiently on God's timing. We have an eternal, good God. Time is on our side.

- Refrain from anger (vv. 8–11). Pity the wicked. They are racing toward their own doom.

Final Thought: The next time you feel frustration at the wicked, trust God instead of becoming angry.

Waiting to Inherit the Earth

Psalm 37:29

"The righteous shall inherit the land, and dwell therein for ever."

God created the world for His people. Satan and his world system currently claim a hold over God's creation, but his time is short. God has already foretold their ultimate defeat and expulsion from the world. In that day, we receive our inheritance.

This truth should lead us to patience. God never makes idle promises. Five times in this psalm, God assures us that in the end we will inherit the earth (vv. 9, 11, 22, 29, 34).

The wicked hold it for a short time, but the righteous will inherit it forever (v. 18). We can joyfully wait for such a day.

This truth also assures us that we'll receive God's provision. David, now an old man, observes in verse 25 that he has never seen God's people without the basic needs of life. We may be awaiting our full inheritance, but God does not wait to provide for the needs of His people.

Final Thought: Wait with joyful expectation, thanking God for daily provision and a world to come.

The Need for Repentance

Psalm 38:18

"For I will declare mine iniquity; I will be sorry for my sin."

No believer walks perfectly on the path of righteousness. Though revived and empowered by Christ, we find our steps dogged by sin. The flesh is weak, and we yield often to its desires. We sin. We stumble out of the way.

But all is not lost. The answer to sin is repentance—turning from our sin back to God's path. Repentance begins by owning our sin. It is "my sin" (v. 3), "my iniquities" (v. 4), and "my foolishness" (v. 5). We need look no further than our own hearts for sin's source. We can't blame anyone else. And the sooner we accept this, the sooner healing can begin.

Our sin brings trouble (v. 6), pain (vv. 7–9), and weakness (v. 10). It separates us from those closest to us (v. 11), and worse, it breaks our fellowship with God (vv. 1–3). This broken walk with God pierced David deeper than all of the other pains together.

In the midst of such sorrow, we find hope in God (v. 15). Only God can provide mercy. And when we call, He hears us. We confess our sin, sorrowing over our gross offense (v. 18). God responds with restored fellowship—a continued salvation. This is the only way we can be restored to the path of righteousness.

Final Thought: Your restoration always comes by way of repentance.

The Path Is Short

Psalm 39:5

"Behold, thou hast made my days as an handbreadth; and mine age is as nothing before thee: verily every man at his best state is altogether vanity."

In first-world countries today, a person's typical lifespan has increased from previous centuries. You likely know someone who has lived to reach 80, 90, or even 100 years of age. Despite the impressive advances in science and medicine, we have barely pushed the average life expectance beyond the 70–80 years mentioned in Psalm 90:10—a mere moment in the history of the world. Compared to the eternality of God, our lives are brief.

When we recognize the brevity of life, our value systems will change. Heaping up possessions and wealth suddenly seems foolish (v. 6). Pursuing the sinful pleasures of this life proves empty (v. 11). Living for this world while neglecting the next makes as much sense as pitching a tent while you wait in line at the grocery store checkout.

Throughout history, God's people have lived as travelers in a foreign land. Paul describes us as soldiers in enemy territory (2 Tim. 2:3–4). In Hebrews 11, the men and women of faith testified by their lives that they were "strangers and pilgrims on the earth" (v. 13). As Christians, we have inherited this legacy. Time is short, but eternity is long. Live as pilgrims.

Final Thought: Are you living with a pilgrim mindset?

The Song of the Forgiven

Psalm 40:3

"And he hath put a new song in my mouth, even praise unto our God: many shall see it, and fear, and shall trust in the LORD."

Private Reynolds lay on the battlefield severely wounded and unable to walk. Swallowed by the clashing of armies, his cry seemed small and ineffective. Suddenly out of the smoke appeared the battle-smeared face of a fellow soldier. The rescuer hefted Reynolds and bore most of his weight as the two shambled back to the safety of camp.

Can you imagine Reynolds's joy at the first sight of his comrade? What must he have felt towards his rescuer?

When we talk about deliverance, we tend to emphasize the "big" events, such as saving a life. But believers have been delivered from an even greater danger than death.

We were sinking in the mire of sin, in the horrible pit of destruction (v. 2a). By His grace, God pulled us out of this wretched condition and set us securely on His path of blessing (v. 2b). This occurs when we place our trust in God alone for our salvation (vv. 3–4).

Such an awesome deliverance should ignite our hearts to praise Him. We have reason to sing a new song, declaring the goodness of God to all who will listen. And as people witness our deliverance and transformation, they will also come to know and reverence this wonderful God.

Final Thought: Sing your new song of praise today.

God, the Theme of Our Song

Psalm 40:10

"I have not hid thy righteousness within my heart; I have declared thy faithfulness and thy salvation: I have not concealed thy lovingkindness and thy truth from the great congregation."

What is David's "new song" that he mentions in Psalm 40:3? It's a song of praise to God. The song begins with the "wonderful works of God" (v. 5). His works are many, so many that counting them defies our best efforts. The thoughts and compassions of God on our behalf would fill every page of every notebook ever produced.

Every "stanza" in a believer's life should point people's eyes upward to God. Our story of deliverance will challenge those around us to trust our Savior. What has God done in your life? How did He bring you to the place of salvation? How has He grown Christ's righteousness in your life since salvation? How has He allowed you to minister for Him?

The character of God fleshes out the song. We could fill hours every day declaring His righteousness, faithfulness, and loving kindness (v. 10). He keeps His thoughts on us to deliver us in His perfect time. When has God provided for you in an unexpected way? How often has His love for you been evidenced? Where would you be without His care?

Final Thought: Magnify the Lord for your deliverance.

The Blessing of Considering Others

Psalm 41:1

"Blessed is he that considereth the poor: the Lord will deliver him in time of trouble."

We live in a world obsessed with self. We're bombarded with advertising messages that tell us a certain product will make us happy or satisfied. Our flesh responds to these messages, trying to find fulfillment in self-satisfaction. But no such pleasures will ever satisfy our flesh.

God calls the people of His way to a different, true blessedness. We find blessing not in the flesh—which is temporary—but in our spirit. We receive this blessing when our lives channel God's love to those around us. The paradox of the Christian life is that as we love and serve others, we ourselves receive blessing.

David presents God as our helper in Psalm 41. God sustains and protects those who willingly serve others in need. He heals the soul when they repent (v. 4). He physically strengthens and gives healing (vv. 2–3, 10). He protects them from their enemies (v. 11). God faithfully preserves those who glorify Him in their service. And when they reach the end of life, these servants receive the ultimate blessing of God's eternal presence.

Final Thought: God preserves His children as they lovingly help those in need.

Where Is Your God?

Psalm 42:11

"Why art thou cast down, O my soul? and why art thou disquieted within me? hope thou in God: for I shall yet praise him, who is the health of my countenance, and my God."

Jesus cried out on the cross, "My God, My God, why have you forsaken me?" These words capture the greatest suffering of the cross—God, the Son, separated from the Godhead as He took our sins on Himself. Because of Christ's suffering, no child of God can be separated from the heavenly Father.

We claim to understand our unbreakable union with God, but our faith falters when we face trouble or God seems distant. Twice in this psalm (v. 3, 10) David records the discouraging taunt from the world—"Where is your God?"

We also struggle at times to fully grasp the reality of our position in Christ. Adversity from the world, our sinful nature, and daily trials discourage us. We thirst. We hunger. Our souls long for what only God can provide. Yet He seems distant.

What is the solution? How do we enjoy the fellowship with God that we know we have? David offers several suggestions:

- Pray, pouring out your soul to God (v. 4a).

- Fellowship, worshipping and praising God with others (v. 4b).

- Meditate, considering God's daily goodness and love (vv. 6–8).

- Hope, trusting that God is near and attentive to all your cares (vv. 5, 11).

Final Thought: Your new life in Christ makes fellowship with God your eternal blessing.

Faith in the Face of Evil

Psalm 43:3

"O send out thy light and thy truth: let them lead me; let them bring me unto thy holy hill, and to thy tabernacles."

We live in a dark world. The way of the ungodly is broad and many travel it, casting a large shadow over the narrow way of the righteous. Psalm 43 continues the theme of Psalm 42—hoping in God despite the world's darkness. Specifically, the psalmist here addresses the ungodly people of this world.

Have you ever stood in an underground cavern without light? If you have, you can probably relate to the psalmist's desire for guidance in verse 3. Someone must provide light and direction. In the darkness of our world, God gives us light and truth to overcome our fear of sin's apparent triumph.

Where will God's light and truth lead us? If we follow, we'll draw closer to Him. We must turn our eyes upon Jesus in answer to our fears. With His presence, God casts out our fears and worries, transforming them into abundant joy and praise (v. 4).

This is my Father's world, O let me ne'er forget
That though the wrong seems oft so strong, God is the ruler yet.
This is my Father's World: the battle is not done!
*Jesus who died shall be satisfied, And earth and Heav'n be one.**

Final Thought: When you feel discouraged, pray for God's light and truth to turn your focus on Him.

*This Is My Father's World, by Maltbie Davenport Babcock. © 1901. Public domain.

The Hero of Your History

Psalm 44:8

"In God we boast all the day long, and praise thy name for ever."

History is exciting. Maybe not the memorization of names and dates, but tales of great heroes and villains from the past grab our imagination. People have told stories of the past for all of human history. To a lesser degree, each of us has a wealth of personal history we enjoy sharing with others. We pass our stories to the next generation.

But who is the hero of your history? For Israel, God was the great hero of history. When Hebrew parents told of the past, the stories enumerated the mighty works of God (v. 2). God had driven out the enemy and freed His people (v. 3). And without God, Israel's future was hopeless (vv. 9–22).

The Jews loved the great fathers of their nation—Abraham, Joseph, David— but these men took second place to God. Their history comprised mere snippets of God's story. Victory was not by sword or human strength; it came from God.

As you tell your stories to the next generation, you too must exalt God to the place He deserves. God provides your needs. God gives strength in your struggles. God gives you wisdom in your pursuits. When your children remember your stories, will they be reminded of the greatness of God?

Final Thought: Your history reveals a story of God's grace.

The King's Bride

Psalm 45:10

"Hearken, O daughter, and consider, and incline thine ear; forget also thine own people, and thy father's house."

Psalm 45 is one of the "royal psalms"—songs that honor the kings of Israel. The New Testament reveals that these psalms prophesied Christ, the great King (see vv. 6–7; Heb. 1:8–9).

This psalm begins with praise for the king. He is handsome and full of gracious words (v. 2). He is powerful (v. 3). He defends truth, meekness, and righteousness (v. 4). He conquers His enemies (v. 5). His rule is eternal (v. 6). His house is full of beauty and pleasure (vv. 8–9).

Then the song shifts from the king to his bride. She is a foreigner, leaving her own nation to become a queen (v. 10). She replaces her old allegiance to her country with a new loyalty to her husband and king (v. 11). Such a replacement is hardly a sacrifice because her new position brings glory, joy, and blessing to both her (vv. 12–15) and her children (vv. 16–17).

This song presents a beautiful picture of our salvation. Christ took us from the kingdom of destruction and brought us by grace into His kingdom. The King welcomes us, not as slaves, but as His beloved bride. And He bestows upon us the blessings of His kingdom—glory, joy, honor, and provision.

Final Thought: Rejoice that Christ is your King and you are His bride.

The Unmoved City

Psalm 46:5

"God is in the midst of her; she shall not be moved: God shall help her, and that right early."

In John Bunyan's classic work, The Pilgrim's Progress, the author contrasts two cities—the Celestial City, which represents heaven, and the city of Vanity Fair, which represents the world.

The fairs of Bunyan's day resembled traveling malls more than the carnivals of today. When the fair arrived in town, vendors would set up booths to sell goods, food, and entertainment. Buying and selling could last for a few days or a few weeks, after which the fair would pack up and move on. Bunyan used the fair to represent the pleasures offered by the world—temporary, always coming and going.

In contrast to the transitory fair, the Celestial City stood on a stone mountain at the end of the King's highway. Only in that place could a pilgrim find eternal joy in the presence of the King.

In the Bible, God used Jerusalem as a similar picture of heaven. The city provided refuge, and the Temple represented God's faithful presence (v. 4). The city's inhabitants enjoyed God's special protection (v. 5).

But Jerusalem offered only a picture of the New Jerusalem—our ultimate dwelling place. At the end of our path, we will rejoice forever in the presence of God, in a city that will never be moved.

Final Thought: Your journey will end at a city built and illuminated by God.

The Sounds of God's Path

Psalm 47:1

"O clap your hands, all ye people; shout unto God with the voice of triumph."

The path of God reverberates with the sounds of praise and worship. Christian hymns and poems speak of God's gracious work on behalf of His people. They proclaim the wisdom and power of Jehovah. They call others to faith in our great God.

As the great King, God triumphs over His enemies (v. 2). He subdues all His enemies (v. 3). He lays claim to the inheritance He has chosen for His people (v. 4).

God's people respond with praise. They clap their hands (v. 1) and shout (vv. 1, 5). They create music with instruments (v. 5) and song (vv. 6–7). With their worship, they exalt their King above all other earthly powers (v. 9).

The psalmist calls on every one of God's people to join in this praise. Whatever gift God has given you can be turned to an act of praise. Whether you produce music in the traditional sense or not, you can still praise Him. Perhaps you are better with your hands than your voice. Then make your labor a song of praise. God delights in both types of sacrifice. And both are a testimony. Our songs and service joyfully declare the greatness of our King.

Final Thought: How are you praising the King today?

Jerusalem, the City of God

Psalm 48:2

"Beautiful for situation, the joy of the whole earth, is mount Zion, on the sides of the north, the city of the great King."

The city of Jerusalem was significant for a number of reasons. One reason for its importance is that God uses the city of Jerusalem to illustrate His character. Here are a few things it reveals about God.

Jerusalem pictured God's strength (vv. 1–3). The surrounding mountains and the city's elevation provided a good defense. Jerusalem's greatness displayed God's supremacy (vv. 4–8). The psalmist paints a picture of the enemy coming to spy on the city's defense, and then fleeing in fear and despair. Jerusalem stood fast because God had established it.

Jerusalem's temple housed God's presence (vv. 9–11). It constantly reminded the city's inhabitants of God's faithful love. God's protection and glory inspired joy.

Our meditation on God's greatness inspires not only praise, but instruction as well. We pass on our praise to the next generation (v. 13), teaching them that God will guide us forever and ever (v. 14).

Final Thought: Great is the Lord, and greatly to be praised.

Fear Not the Rich

Psalm 49:8

"For the redemption of their soul is precious, and it ceaseth for ever."

Money seems to solve every earthly problem, giving people protection and power. People praise and honor the wealthy because of their power. But Psalm 49 reminds believers of the things money cannot do.

First, money cannot purchase eternal life. The price of a soul far exceeds any accumulated wealth (vv. 7–9). The grave is their final end, but God will ransom those who trust in Him (v. 15).

Second, money cannot secure a family's heritage. The wealthy may use money to establish their family's future, naming businesses, cities, or even nations after themselves (v. 11). Yet they die. Even though following generations may carry on the founder's reputation (v. 13), those generations will also pass away.

Third, money cannot accompany the rich after death. Although money is a blessing in this life, its power ends at the grave (v. 17). David states that the person who fails to understand money's limitations is no better than a mindless beast (v. 20).

Final Thought: Place your trust in God, not in your material resources.

Two Offerings of Our Mouth

Psalm 50:23

"Whoso offereth praise glorifieth me: and to him that ordereth his conversation aright will I shew the salvation of God."

In this psalm, David presents God coming to judge both His people and the wicked (vv. 3–4, 16). God addresses His people first. He rebukes them, not for their offering, but for their wrong attitudes (vv. 7–8, 14). God states that He does not need their offerings, because He owns every beast of the forest and the cattle on a thousand hills (vv. 10–12).

What kind of offering does God desire? He wants the sacrifice of thankfulness and sincerity (vv. 14–15). He listens for our desperate prayers of faith. God desires a right heart attitude more than material sacrifice.

The offerings that pour from the mouth of the wicked reveal their heart as well. They despise the instruction of God's Word (v. 17). They prefer the company of thieves and adulterers—those who do not give, but steal (v. 18). Instead of praise, they speak evil words and lies, slandering even their own brother (vv. 19–20).

When God comes to judge, He will evaluate our words, not the content of our sacrifices (vv. 21, 23). For it is out of the heart our mouths speak. A heart changed by the grace of salvation will produce gratitude and praise.

Final Thought: Let your words be a sacrifice of thanksgiving to God.

Only God Can Cleanse Us

Psalm 51:7

"Purge me with hyssop, and I shall be clean: wash me, and I shall be whiter than snow."

No honest person can deny that he or she sins. Our sin nature is knotted inextricably into the fabric of our identity. Broken relationships, failed dreams, and disappointments remind us daily of the effects of our sin. Yet the sorrows that sin brings us cannot compare to the offense that our sin gives to God.

The God that we've rejected is the only one Who can change our sin nature. In this psalm, David repeatedly reminds the reader that God must do the work of cleansing. He entreats God's mercy and requests God to erase our record of sin (v. 1). God will wash us and purge out the stain (vv. 2, 7). He will hide His face from our sins (v. 9). He will create a clean heart and renew our spirit in us (v. 10), and restore the joy of His path (v. 12).

The wonderful news is that God delights to cleanse us and change our nature. Because God loves us unconditionally, He desires to remove our sin. He sent His Son into the world for this very cause—to save sinners. We come to God with brokenness and humility for our sins, but we also come with boldness because of Christ. God readily receives our requests, because He never despises the repentant sinner.

Final Thought: You will always find forgiveness when you confess your sins to God.

A Spiritual Greenhouse

Psalm 52:8

"But I am like a green olive tree in the house of God: I trust in the mercy of God for ever and ever."

Greenhouses provide a controlled environment for young plants to grow safely—even if outdoor conditions are inhospitable. A wise gardener maintains the correct temperature, moisture, and nutrients to grow healthy plants.

David compares himself, and all believers, to a green olive tree planted in God's house. The Father faithfully and lovingly cares for the young tree. He guards it and allows only those things that will help to create a strong, fruitful plant—a spiritually mature Christian on God's path.

The wicked do not plant themselves in the house of God. They reject God's Word and pursue their own desires. They take root in their own schemes (vv. 1–2) and lies (vv. 2–3). They love evil more than good (v. 3). This kind of cultivation may look healthy for a while, but God will uproot them out of the land of the living (v. 5).

Final Thought: Place yourself under God's care, for He is good.

Our Ways All Fail

Psalm 53:3

"Every one of them is gone back: they are altogether become filthy; there is none that doeth good, no, not one."

People repeatedly attempt to create good without God. Social programs and religions promise to deliver benefits and fulfillment. Yet history contains a graveyard of these efforts marred by corruption, folly, and sin.

Albert Einstein defined insanity as doing the same thing over and over while expecting different results. In this sense, the human race engages in a shared insanity. We continually depend on humans and human institutions to reverse the effects of sin, when only God has the ability to do so.

God has searched the hearts of people. He has examined every plan and motive, every thought and word. He concludes that everyone falls away into corruption. Because of our sin nature, we're unable to please God or obey Him by our own effort. Theologians call this human depravity.

No one enjoys the effects of sin. We see the effects of depravity—such as violence, hatred, and death—around us in every area of life. Yet we have hope. In Romans 3:23, Paul acknowledges that everyone has sinned. But in verse 24, he points to our hope—the gift of salvation through the unmerited goodness of God. Christ offers the solution to the sin problem shared by all of humanity.

Final Thought: Don't look to people for things that only God can provide.

Taking Time to Praise After Deliverance

Psalm 54:6

"I will freely sacrifice unto thee: I will praise thy name, O LORD; for it is good."

We encounter many trials while traveling on God's path, and they can easily become the consuming focus of our prayers. Our difficulties are real, and God encourages us to cast our cares on Him. David devoted many psalms to prayers of deliverance, but he also offers praise for God's response.

Our thanksgiving tends to lack the urgency that our prayers for deliverance possess. Often we neglect to give thanks at all—a problem shared by many. The Israelites experienced miraculous deliverance from Egypt, yet they grumbled constantly. Ten lepers received healing from Jesus, but only one returned to express thanks. In Romans 1, Paul states that people's rejection of God's revelation involves two sins—a failure to glorify God and a failure to give thanks to Him (v. 21).

As believers, we owe God thanks for so much. He created us and gave us the capability to enjoy Him. He sent His Son to pay the price of our salvation. He provides for His people. He delivers us from sin's bondage. Because everything we receive from God is good, we have every reason to thank Him.

David goes beyond merely thanking God to fulfill a duty. He offers gratitude and praise freely as a voluntary offering. Overwhelmed by the goodness of his God, David allows thanks to flow naturally from his lips. Here lies the key to a truly thankful heart. Thankfulness doesn't come from force of will—"I will be thankful." It comes instead through meditation on the character, goodness, and works of God.

Final Thought: Meditate on God's deliverance and let grateful praise fill your prayers to Him.

Fleeing to God

Psalm 55:6

"And I said, Oh that I had wings like a dove! For then would I fly away, and be at rest."

Today's passage reveals David in danger once more from enemy attack. We'll look at the unique nature of this attack tomorrow, but today we will focus on David's desire for relief—a desire we've all experienced.

Consider how serious this trial was for David. Enemies devised vengeful plans for the king's destruction (v. 3). David felt sick with the fear of death (v. 4), and he trembled at the mounting horror of the attack (v. 5). David is not alone, for we all have experienced similar reactions to certain trials.

David had a strong desire to escape his storm (vv. 6–8), but there was no way to evade it. He felt its continual presence upon his heart and mind.

What could David do? The wilderness granted no peace. Only one place remained for David, and he fled to God. That night he prayed. In the morning, He woke with prayer on his lips and continued in prayer throughout the day (v. 17). He could not escape the trial, but he could rest in his God. God had delivered his soul before, and God could do it again.

Many Christians live in countries where their faith places them in constant danger. Others live with daily struggles such as disease, violence, broken relationships, and the haunting memories of abuse. Like David, we wish to find refuge away from these trials, but we can't escape them. Though we must face the enemy, we find peace in God's present help. God is our true refuge.

Final Thought: Cry to the Lord at any time of day or night—He will hear you!

When Friends Fail Us

Psalm 55:12

"For it was not an enemy that reproached me; then I could have borne it: neither was it he that hated me that did magnify himself against me; then I would have hid myself from him."

Yesterday we read about David's desire to escape his terrible trial. It's as if David pled, "Let me wake up and find all this was just a nightmare." The nature of this particular attack brought greater pain to David. His enemies were not strangers—they were David's dear friends, led by his own son.

Absalom, David's estranged son, decided he should be king and that David wasn't dying fast enough. He led a coup against King David in the capital city of Jerusalem, forcing the king to flee for his life. Some of David's friends fled with him, but others betrayed him by joining the coup. Psalm 55 likely refers to Ahithophel, David's friend and counselor, and one of his "mighty men" (1 Chron. 27:33–34). The man joined forces with Absalom and encouraged him to pursue and kill David (2 Sam. 15–17). No wonder David felt his sorrow and fear so poignantly.

Have you ever known the betrayal of a dear friend in your time of need? Have you known the sorrow of betrayal and desertion? If so, look to the Lord. In Christ, we have a true friend who sticks closer than a brother. He knows what you are experiencing. He also endured the betrayal of a close friend. Jesus knows your sorrow, and He invites you to call on Him for help.

Final Thought: Friends may forsake you, but God will never leave.

Our Defense Against Fear

Psalm 56:3

"What time I am afraid, I will trust in thee."

Faith provides the only means to pass through the dangers that close in around us. Our own resources—strength, wealth, friends, wisdom—can't calm our fears. Only through faith can we experience true deliverance from our fear.

But faith in God is not some vague feeling. It is trust in God's promises to His people. These promises include:

- God will never forsake you (Heb. 13:5).

- God withholds no good thing from you (Ps. 84:11).

- God will answer your prayer according to His will (Matt. 7:7).

- God keeps and sustains you (Ps. 55:22).

- God provides you with good and perfect gifts (James 1:17).

- God is preparing a home for you in heaven (John 14:2–3).

- God delivers you from evil (Gal. 1:4).

God's Word offers many promises to calm our fears. God is for us. Who can stand against us? God controls everything that comes into our lives. He allows only those troubles that help shape us for our good and His glory.

Final Thought: Meditate on God's promises to overcome your fears.

God's High Glory

Psalm 57:5

"Be thou exalted, O God, above the heavens; let thy glory be above all the earth."

Children, in their simplicity, imagine that God lives up in the sky. Heaven drifts among the clouds, just out of view. As their understanding grows, they realize that the heavenly realm is larger than the sky. God's abode encompasses even the far reaches of space.

But even the vastness of the universe cannot hold the God revealed in Scripture. God is exalted above the heavens. The expanse of creation cannot contain Him and His glory (v. 5).

David responds to this exalted vision of God in two ways. In the first stanza, David says he will cry out to God (v. 2). Though God is exalted above the heavens, He hears the cries of His people and responds in love and faithfulness. The exalted God lovingly helps the humble saint.

In the second stanza, David sings praises to his exalted God (vv. 7–9). He wakes early to welcome the dawn with praise (v. 8). He sings of the expansive, merciful love of God and His truth, which reaches above all this world's falsehood (v. 10). He praises God among the nations to direct their eyes upward (v. 9).

Final Thought: Let us praise our exalted God.

Surely There Is a God Who Judges

Psalm 58:11

"So that a man shall say, Verily there is a reward for the righteous: verily he is a God that judgeth in the earth."

The wicked appear powerful. Throughout our world, they oppress, exploit, and destroy others. Their ways overflow with poison and violence. They refuse to listen to God's rebuke and instruction. David compares them to a poisonous snake that will not be charmed (vv. 4–5). They multiply and practice their natural sinfulness, becoming experts in their rebellion.

But David doesn't stop with merely comparing the wicked to snakes. The wicked are also like lions, but God will break their teeth (v. 6). They are like bows of war, but God will break and blunt their arrows (v. 7). They will be like slugs melted by salt (v. 8a). Like a miscarriage, their plans will not come to fruition (v. 8b).

God judges and overthrows the rebellion of wicked that the righteous may see and rejoice in His power (v. 10). The path of the wicked ends in destruction, as must every path that does not lead to God through Christ. Christ taught this exclusivity when He stated that He alone provides the way, the truth, and the life (John 14:6). God's judgment of the wicked reveals that He will cut off those who reject His way.

Final Thought: You can be confident that the Judge of all the earth will do right.

The Laugh of God

Psalm 59:8

"But thou, O LORD, shalt laugh at them; thou shalt have all the heathen in derision."

A strong enemy's laughter strikes dread in the hearts of the hearers. It shows a disdain for opposition, certain that any effort against the enemy will fail. The army of Israel quaked with dread at the mocking laughter of Goliath (1 Sam 17:11). But the giant's mocking held no fear for David. The young man knew that God in heaven laughed at Goliath's pathetic challenge.

David repeatedly writes of God laughing at the wicked (v. 8; 2:4; 37:13). God doesn't fear their schemes. If all the wicked united to oppose God, they would fall at a single command from God. They have no hope of victory.

Why then does God allow the wicked to prosper? Why doesn't He judge them immediately?

God has a plan for them. He allows the consequences of their evil to destroy them (v. 11). He demolishes their plans and traps them in their pride (v. 12). The destructive fruit of wickedness glorifies the righteous path of God's people. We were once part of that futile rebellion, but God saved us. God faces no true opposition.

Final Thought: Thank the Lord and rejoice in the certainty of His power.

From Defeat to Deliverance

Psalm 60:1

"O God, thou hast cast us off, thou hast scattered us, thou hast been displeased; O turn thyself to us again."

In this psalm, David reflects on one of his battles to consolidate his power in Israel. He expected an easy victory, but the rebellious Edomites had repelled David's first attack. David reveals the cause of his failure in verses 10–12—he had not trusted God. His army had trusted in its own strength, rejecting God's help. As a result, God allowed the enemy to scatter David's army (v. 1).

From this experience, David learned that humankind's strength is powerless without God (v. 11). Only in God can we achieve victory (v. 12). God controls the outcome of every battle. When we fight in our own strength, we try to wrest that control from God, producing disastrous results.

We have all failed during the course of our lives. We fail repeatedly when we try to resist sin with only our own strength. We are too weak. The world, the devil, and our flesh easily overcome us, and discouragement follows.

Thankfully, God will not leave us defeated. He allows hard things so that we can retreat to His banner (vv. 3–4), the place of deliverance (v. 5).

As we return to God and trust Him, He will restore us (v. 1); He heals the breaches (v. 2). He saves us (v. 5). He hears our prayers (v. 5), and He gives help (v. 11).

Final Thought: Use your failures as reminders to depend on God for healing and deliverance.

The Pattern of Prayer

Psalm 61:2

"From the end of the earth will I cry unto thee, when my heart is overwhelmed: lead me to the rock that is higher than I."

Many of David's psalms echo his life struggles and hardships. In his seventy years, he faced:

- His brother's ridicule
- Saul's murderous wrath
- Exile
- The death of a dear friend
- The rape of his daughter by her half-brother
- His son's murder
- A coup led by a son
- The death of several of his children
- Betrayal by close friends

No one would view such a life as desirable, but God used all these hardships to encourage David's trust in Him. David expresses this trust in the songs and prayers we know and love.

David often followed a pattern of prayer containing four parts. Let's look briefly at each of these parts in Psalm 61.

- David cried unto the Lord (vv. 1–2). He never hesitated to take his needs to his faithful and loving God.

- David waited on the Lord (vv. 3–4a). He ran first to the Lord and looked only to Him for help.

- David trusted in the Lord (vv. 4b–7). He believed that God had heard his prayer and would act on his behalf. David waited patiently for an answer.

- David praised the Lord (v. 8). He sang to God for the help and answers he received. He often praised the Lord even before receiving an answer to his prayer.

Final Thought: When faced with trials, cry out to God and trust Him.

A Higher Rock

Psalm 61:4

"I will abide in thy tabernacle for ever: I will trust in the cover of thy wings."

One of our greatest needs is spiritual shelter—protection from forces that harm us. And we need greater shelter than we can provide for ourselves. Too often we face life in our own strength, like trying to shelter ourselves from a hurricane with only an umbrella. God wants these storms to force our eyes upward, where we find a "higher rock" (v. 2). God is our rock, giving us solid footing as we travel our spiritual path.

William Cushing captures this truth in his hymn "Hiding in Thee."

O safe to the Rock that is higher than I,
My soul in its conflicts and sorrows would fly;
Alone I would perish, undone would I be;
Thou blest "Rock of Ages," I'm hiding in Thee.

Refrain:

Hiding in Thee, hiding in Thee,
Thou blest "Rock of Ages," I'm hiding in Thee.

In the calm of the noontide, in sorrow's lone hour,
In times when temptation casts o'er me its pow'r;
In the tempests of life, on its wide, heaving sea,
Thou blest "Rock of Ages," I'm hiding in Thee.

How oft in the conflict, when pressed by the foe,
I have fled to my Refuge and breathed out my woe;
How often, when trials like sea billows roll,
Have I hidden in Thee, O Thou Rock of my soul.

Final Thought: When overwhelmed and ready to faint, find strength and help in God.

God, Our Only True Help

Psalm 62:2

"He only is my rock and my salvation; he is my defence; I shall not be greatly moved."

As Christians, we approach God not because He is the best help available, but because He is the only help. We have no other way of salvation, no other defense against the enemy, no other help as we walk the way of the righteous. Only God is a firm foundation (vv. 2, 6).

The world offers its own help, but this help fails. Whether highborn or low, people cannot offer lasting help (v. 9). Riches—gained through violence or peace—seem to offer security, but ultimately prove empty (v. 10).

God is exclusive and jealous. He does not tolerate other gods in our lives. Because God alone possesses true power (v. 11), we sin by looking for power in anyone or anything else.

John Newton captured this truth powerfully in his well-known hymn, "Amazing Grace." The third and fourth stanzas speak of God's gracious help in this life.

Through many dangers, toils and snares,
I have already come;
'Tis grace hath brought me safe thus far,
And grace will lead me home.

The Lord has promised good to me,
His Word my hope secures;
He will my Shield and Portion be,
As long as life endures.

Final Thought: Find your help in God alone.

A Thirsty Path

Psalm 63:1

"O God, thou art my God; early will I seek thee: my soul thirsteth for thee, my flesh longeth for thee in a dry and thirsty land, where no water is."

When extreme thirst attacks our senses, we can think of little else. Water is crucial to our survival, so when it gets low, our bodies signal us to address the problem.

David, writing this psalm while hiding in the Judean wilderness, understood physical thirst. Water was rare in this barren land between Jerusalem and the Jordan. But this physical thirst mirrored a deeper, spiritual thirst—the thirst of every believer for God. Every Christian traveler experiences this thirst as he or she passes through the world. Like intense longing for water, a desire for God consumes our thoughts even when we rise in the morning (v. 1) and lie down at night (v. 6).

We ache to experience God's power and glory (v. 2). We long to inhabit the places of worship (v. 2b). We find true satisfaction only when we find Him. And when we are satisfied, our lips naturally sing His praises (v. 5). The world can offer nothing to fill our desire for God.

Once a person truly experiences the help and satisfaction of God, he despairs of all other earthly pleasures. He may pursue the pleasures, but they always end hollow and tasteless. With David, he must confess that the joy of God is "better than life" (v. 3). He finds true rest only in the shadow of God's wings (v. 7).

Final Thought: Spend time today drinking in the power and glory of God.

God's Glory in Destroying the Wicked

Psalm 64:9

"And all men shall fear, and shall declare the work of God; for they shall wisely consider of his doing."

Many people in history have chosen the path of wickedness because it promised success in some way—theft brings wealth, boasting brings promotion, war brings power. But the wicked follow a path that ends in destruction. Because of His character, God cannot tolerate sin. If He didn't exist, we could expect sinners to successfully avoid the consequences of sin. But God does exist, so He will not allow sin to go unpunished (v. 7).

And in overthrowing the wicked, God receives glory. He turns their plans against them. When this happens, the observers respond in three ways (v. 8–9).

People fear God's law. Even if they fail to fear God Himself, they understand that wrongdoing brings undesirable consequences and that righteousness brings reward.

People declare the judgment of God. Every day, we're confronted by news of people reaping the consequences of their sins.

People reflect on their own choices. They observe their own cycle of sin and judgment and may take it into account when making decisions.

Although God's judgment should prompt people to learn from it and reject sinful temptation, many of us continue to make sinful choices and risk the consequences. Those who turn from God may have temporary success, but God will ultimately glorify Himself by judging them. God intends His glorious judgment to direct people from their sin to the cross.

Final Thought: Praise God for His judgment on sin.

The Satisfaction of Dwelling with God

Psalm 65:4

"Blessed is the man whom thou choosest, and causest to approach unto thee, that he may dwell in thy courts: we shall be satisfied with the goodness of thy house, even of thy holy temple."

The path of the righteous ends in the bountiful courts of God. In John Bunyan's masterful allegory, The Pilgrim's Progress, Christian anticipates and often speaks of the end of his dangerous journey at the Celestial City. Every pilgrim in this world shares that hope. But what will this new heaven and new earth be like?

In Psalm 65, David contemplates the blessedness of dwelling in God's presence. He then lists the amazing works of God in this world. God has firmly established the lofty mountains (v. 6) and restrained the roaring oceans (v. 7). The rising and setting sun rejoices in God's created splendor (v. 8). He provides rain and an abundance of crops (vv. 9–11) and spreads out green pastures filled with livestock and crops (vv. 12–13).

At first glance, David's shift from the blessing of God's presence to God's creation may seem strange. But consider for a moment what these wondrous works indicate about heaven. The God who created the majestic mountains and restrains the raging oceans is preparing a new heaven and a new earth. The wonders of our world are mere shadows of the wonders to come. God will build a city with glorious gemstones that will make this world's sunsets pale in comparison. And the bounty of this world's harvests and flocks dimly hint at the glorious provision of our heavenly home.

Final Thought: As you consider God's works in this world, remember that greater glory waits in His presence.

Purposeful Praise

Psalm 66:5

"Come and see the works of God: he is terrible in his doing toward the children of men."

Previously, we learned that God's people praise Him. Today, we'll look at several purposes of praise.

First and foremost, we praise as a sacrifice to God, the only one worthy of our praise. Today's psalm introduces a second purpose of our praise—to call others to worship God.

On a mundane level, we often use praise to draw attention to something. We may rave over the food at our favorite restaurant, hoping to get others to try it. We may describe the artistic merit of some book or movie, expecting our friends to check it out. Our praise often inspires a response from others.

Our praise of God likewise impacts other people's attention and evokes a response. We praise God for the glory and honor of His name—the essence of who He is (v. 2). We declare the power of His works—both natural and supernatural (v. 3). We share how He has worked in our lives, sustaining us, testing us, chastening us, and blessing us (vv. 8–12). We confess how God has heard our cry for forgiveness and answered our prayers (vv. 16–20).

God gives glory to such praise and uses it to draw others to Himself.

Final Thought: Infuse your worship and witness with praise to the Lord.

Blessed for God's Glory

"God shall bless us; and all the ends of the earth shall fear him."

God does all things with purpose. Because He intends our praise to draw people to Him (Ps. 66), He blesses us so that we can glorify Him. God gives love and mercy for our good (Rom. 8:28) and for His glory.

Because people learn about God through our praise, we must respond to God's blessings in a way that reflects God's character. We must not claim to have earned God's blessings, thereby stealing His glory for ourselves. We must not hoard God's blessings like the man who built bigger barns (Luke 12:18), but instead we share our blessings so others can see what God has done and praise Him with us. Even our enjoyment of God's blessings testifies to the goodness of our God.

God causes His face to shine upon you for your good and for His glory. He also intends His blessings to reach others through you.

Jesus taught this truth in His earthly ministry. In Matthew 10, He sends forth His disciples to minister to the cities of Israel. These followers had received the blessings of Jesus' teaching and power. Jesus says to them, "The things you have received, go now and give them to others" (v. 8).

This principle also appears in God's covenant with Abraham (Gen. 26:3–4). God promised to bless Abraham and, through him, all the nations of the world.

Final Thought: Reflect the goodness and glory of God to others by your praise.

God's Compassion for the Lonely

Psalm 68:5

"A father of the fatherless, and a judge of the widows, is God in his holy habitation."

God has great compassion on those who have been abandoned in life. James even writes that true, pure worship involves helping those who have been abandoned (James 1:27). In verse 5 of Psalm 68, God declares Himself to be the Father who cares for the fatherless, and the Judge who defends the rights of widows. When we lose loved ones in this world—a parent, spouse, or child—God takes a special interest in our care.

Not only does God protect and provide, but He also blesses us with comfort from our brothers and sisters in Christ (v. 6). As a reflection of Christ, believers welcome the brokenhearted and encourage the lonely. They care for them, even to the point of adopting children into Christian homes or treating strangers like family.

In Christ, we have a bond stronger than family relations. We should reach out to the hurting as instruments of God's compassion. When we feel lonely, we can rest in God's loving arms and in the care of other believers.

Final Thought: Care for those around you and show them the compassion of God.

Bearing God's Burden

Psalm 69:7

"Because for thy sake I have borne reproach; shame hath covered my face."

We read in Scripture that God gives strength to help us bear our burdens. Not only do we face the trials of living in a fallen world, but we also bear a part of God's burden—the rejection and hostility that the world hurls at God.

David discovered that as he became consumed with God, people mocked and attacked him with increasing frequency. People who hated God (v. 9), as well as those in high positions (v. 12), reproached him. Even the drunkards made up songs to mock him (v. 12). Just as these people attacked God, they also attacked God's servant.

People still attack God's servants today, simply for the fact that they identify with God. Jesus warned His disciples that they should expect persecution (Matt. 5:10–12). The world crucified our Master, so we should expect similar treatment when we follow Him.

Jesus states that we should respond to this treatment with rejoicing. We identify as the children of a powerful, loving God. We share in the burden of His reproach for a time, but we will also share in the reward of His heaven for all eternity.

Final Thought: Rejoice that you can bear a part of the reproach of Christ.

Why Does God Listen?

Psalm 69:16

"Hear me, O LORD; for thy lovingkindness is good: turn unto me according to the multitude of thy tender mercies."

Humans have a tendency to manipulate others to get what they want from them. This often carries over into prayer. Many people attempt to control the outcome of their prayer requests by offering a gift, achieving a heightened spiritual state, or making a vow.

Occasionally, the ancient Romans practiced a ritual in which a general would sacrifice himself to Mars—the god of war—for a favorable outcome in battle. The Philistines—and even the Israelites (Judges 10:6)—offered sacrifices to false gods like Baal, a god of fertility, to ensure a good harvest.

Today, we may not offer animal sacrifice or make vows, but sometimes we try to earn God's favor with our actions. The God of the Bible accepts no such bribes. In Psalm 50, God states that He has no need for the gifts that people give. He weighs only the heart attitude that inspires such gifts. So if we can't buy God's answer, how can we guarantee that God will hear and answer our prayers?

David provides an answer not in our actions, but in God's character (vv. 13, 16). God hears and answers us for the sake of His steadfast love and immeasurable mercies. We have hope in prayer because our God delights in answering His children.

Final Thought: Pray with confidence, because God hears those that call on Him.

God's Help in My Need

Psalm 70:5

"But I am poor and needy: make haste unto me, O God: thou art my help and my deliverer; O LORD, make no tarrying."

Hebrew poetry contains parallelism. Instead of rhyming words, the poets would rhyme ideas. Sometimes they would simply repeat the same idea:

> "Make haste, O God, to deliver me
> Make haste to help me, O Lord" (v. 1).

Other times they would use a second line to expand the first line:

"Let all those that seek thee rejoice and be glad in thee and let such as love thy salvation say continually, Let God be magnified" (v. 4).

In today's verse, the psalmist uses a third type of parallelism—the second line shows the flip side of the first.

Notice that David's request in both lines remains the same. He calls upon God to act quickly and not to delay. But the rest of the verse shows the reason for David's prayer. First, he recognizes his condition. He acknowledges that he is poor and needy. But then he turns his eyes to God, and declares that God is a help and deliverer. God provides the only kind of help that will meet his need.

Final Thought: Lord, I am needy, but You are my absolute and constant help.

Three Enemies of God

Psalm 71:4

"Deliver me, O my God, out of the hand of the wicked, out of the hand of the unrighteous and cruel man."

David often prays for deliverance from the enemies of God. In today's verse, David names three of these enemies. Though these enemies manifest themselves differently over the years, all three still exist, and we still need God's deliverance from them.

The wicked find pleasure in immorality (Prov. 1:10–16; Rom. 1:32). They seek to satisfy themselves with sin and the lusts of this world. They also urge others to join them in sin.

The unrighteous resist God's justice (Prov. 14:9). They defy any attempts to establish absolute right and wrong. They attack God's Word and God's people, often describing them as narrow, unenlightened, and intolerant.

The cruel delight in harming others (Prov. 12:10). They lack compassion. Sin has so twisted their hearts and minds that they take pleasure in causing or observing pain in others.

God alone is our defense against such people. They are children of their father, the devil, and they will share his fate.

Final Thought: Though we face terrible foes, God remains in sovereign control.

God, a Help in Old Age

Psalm 71:9

"Cast me not off in the time of old age; forsake me not when my strength faileth."

Much of modern culture tends to idolize youth and superficial beauty at the expense of age and inner beauty. But God does not share this mindset. He is faithful to the young and the old alike.

David wrote Psalm 71 in the later years of his life (v. 9). Physical health had begun to fail him. His days of strength and battle faded away, and his generals begged him to stay home in war time (2 Sam. 21:15–17). Because David neared the end of his life, people began plotting to take his place.

But David remembered the faithfulness of God throughout his life (vv. 17–18). God had taught his hand to war, and God would continue to sustain him to the end.

God gives each of us a certain time on this earth. Though our strength eventually fades, God does not change. If you have reached the later part of life, trust in His continued provision. If you are still young, act as God's tools of compassion to elderly saints.

Final Thought: The God of your youth will remain faithful into your twilight years.

Prayer for the Next Generation

Psalm 72:1

"Give the king thy judgments, O God, and thy righteousness unto the king's son."

We have a burden to prepare our children for the future. We teach them through stories, financial guidance, and warnings. As Christians, prayer makes up a major part of that preparation. In Psalm 72, David offers a prayer for future kingship of his son, Solomon.

David recognized that for future success, Solomon required blessing from God. He would need wisdom and righteousness as he led God's people (v. 2). He would need God's provision for his people's prosperity to continue (v. 3). Finally, he would need God's love working in him to give mercy to the needy and justice to the oppressor (v. 4).

When we pray for our children and those we teach or lead, our prayer should reflect David's. God expects us to do our part in passing on these things, but ultimately we recognize that God must work. When we teach the things of God to the next generation, we have passed on something far greater than any earthly treasure.

Final Thought: How are you passing on a passion for God to the next generation?

The Danger of Envying the Wicked

Psalm 73:3

"For I was envious at the foolish, when I saw the prosperity of the wicked."

In Psalm 73, Asaph records a struggle that assaults every Christian's heart at some point in his or her journey. We have chosen the straight and narrow way of the righteous. This path certainly has its struggles and dangers. And as we struggle along our path, we observe a difference in those who have chosen the other path—a road without thought for God.

Those who have rejected God and His way seem to prosper. They avoid many of the struggles that the saints have to endure. By cunning and deceit they heap up wealth. With violence they destroy people in their way. By ignoring God they appear to enjoy more free time and less constraints. They appear to travel a smooth road lined with ease and prosperity.

When we are tempted to envy them, we must learn the lesson of Asaph. First, we are only glimpsing a single scene in the lives of these people. Whatever the moment holds, they are on a path of ultimate destruction. Second, their current pleasures don't last. Asaph saw that they stood on slippery places (v. 18). Like Moses, he recognized that the pleasures of sin are only for a season (Heb. 11:25). Third, they can never find the most important thing—a relationship with God—in all of their pleasure (vv. 25–26).

Final Thought: Never envy those who have no relationship with God, no matter how prosperous they seem.

The Empty Celebration of the Wicked

Psalm 74:10

"O God, how long shall the adversary reproach? Shall the enemy blaspheme thy name for ever?"

Over the centuries, many wicked people have attempted to end Christianity. Many Roman emperors, culminating with Diocletian, tried to stamp out the early Church in its infancy. But the numbers of believers only swelled, increased by some of the very people sent to persecute the church. Barbarian tribes of the Middle Ages slaughtered many believers and unbelievers alike. Even in recent centuries, many governments and organizations have tried to expel Christianity from their country's borders.

Often in these persecutions and attacks, wicked leaders declared their triumph over Christianity. The philosopher Voltaire believed that the growth of human knowledge would lead to the eradication of Christianity among the educated class. Adolf Hitler declared that his National Socialism and Christianity could not coexist. Yet such boasts always prove false.

Unlike followers of a national or political power, Christians are bound by a spiritual power that defies eradication. Though we face opposition—and sometimes even death—for our faith, God will continue to call people to follow and worship Him. Our enemies cannot triumph, because God has the victory.

Final Thought: No matter what opposition you may face, our sovereign, powerful God will preserve His message.

Allow God to Exalt You

Psalm 75:7

"But God is the judge: he putteth down one, and setteth up another."

In our world, people step on each other to get ahead. Something in our nature wants to be in first place. You'll never find a mug that reads, "World's 4th Best Dad." As far as most people are concerned, second place is just first loser.

Motivated by this mindset, the world uses people and things to help them get ahead. Another degree from a prestigious school might bring about that next promotion. Befriend the boss's kids to get in good with an employer. Buy some new device or flashy car to impress friends. Do whatever it takes to get noticed and get ahead. It's a rat race, and everyone wants to be the first place rat.

In Psalm 75, Asaph points to a better way. He warns about the futility of self-promotion in the world. He cautions against tooting our own horn, drawing attention to personal prowess (vv. 4–5). He declares that we can seek promotion from any number of places, but all are fruitless apart from God (vv. 6–7).

Instead we should build habits of gratitude, thanking God for His work in our lives (v. 1). God has placed you where you are. Rejoice and serve Him there. Humble yourself before God, and He will exalt you in His time and for His purpose (vv. 9–10).

Final Thought: You can depend upon God to exalt you in His time.

God Receives Glory from Everything

Psalm 76:10

"Surely the wrath of man shall praise thee: the remainder of wrath shalt thou restrain."

Goliath. Sennacherib. Nebuchadnezzar. Herod. All of these men have something in common—they each defied God and desired glory for themselves. As such, we wouldn't expect them to be on a list of people who praise God.

Yet the Bible makes clear that everything—even the hostility of the world—ultimately gives praise to God (Phil. 2:10–11). How does God accomplish this?

God receives glory because He can accomplish what no one else can. The destruction of Goliath and Sennacherib, along with their respective followers, demonstrated the power of God. Nebuchadnezzar's conversion and song of praise to the Lord testified to God's ability to change hearts (Dan. 4:34–37). Herod attempted the murder of Jesus, but God turned his plans to the greatest event of human history.

Today, God still receives glory through similar ways—destroying, converting, and frustrating His enemies. God's sovereignty guarantees that He will not allow any evil that does not give Him glory.

Final Thought: Don't fear God's enemies, because God will turn their actions into His glory.

The Remedy of Remembering

Psalm 77:11

"I will remember the works of the LORD: surely I will remember thy wonders of old."

In Psalm 77, Asaph recounts a deep physical and spiritual struggle he had faced. Nothing could comfort his constant, intense suffering (v. 2). Even meditating upon God brought only groaning and despair (v. 3). Sleep fled from him (v. 4a), and he couldn't express his suffering in words (v. 4b). In discouragement, he questioned God's care and compassion (vv. 7–9).

How did Asaph handle his burden? The answer comes in the middle of the psalm. He turns his eyes from the sufferings of the moment and remembers the blessings he has enjoyed as God's child (vv. 10–13). He recalls the days of rich blessing at God's right hand and the wonderful works of God on his behalf. God had worked daily for the good of His children. The suffering of the moment did not reflect the totality of God's works.

He also thinks of God's love and mercy to the people of Israel (vv. 15, 20). The power of God turned gently to the aid of His children. He ruled over all nature for their good. Triumph replaced his despair when he meditated on God's goodness.

Final Thought: Find comfort in your trials by remembering the past goodness of God.

Our Obligation to the Next Generation

Psalm 78:4

"We will not hide them from their children, shewing to the generation to come the praises of the LORD, and his strength, and his wonderful works that he hath done."

God commands each generation to teach the subsequent generation. The brevity of life means that what is not passed on will eventually vanish from memory. While God's Word remains forever, we must teach it to our children to introduce them to God.

God mentions in this verse three types of things we should teach to the next generation. First, we must relate the praiseworthy character of God. We testify of how God reflects His character in His actions. Many Christian hymns focus on God's works and character, making them great tools for encouraging devotion in children.

Second, we talk about God's might. We teach children that God is all-powerful. No one can resist His plans or will. This knowledge gives us confidence to replace our fear and anxiety. There exists no greater remedy for the fears of childhood.

Third, we talk of God's wonders. Teaching these miraculous works of God on behalf of His people gives peace and hope to the next generation. If God has answered prayer in the past, we can go to Him expecting Him to continue to answer.

Take every opportunity to declare the glories of God to the children God has placed in your life.

Final Thought: What are you passing on to the next generation?

Teaching from Our Mistakes

Psalm 78:8

"And might not be as their fathers, a stubborn and rebellious generation; a generation that set not their heart aright, and whose spirit was not stedfast with God."

Last time, we looked at our responsibility to teach the next generation about God. The second part of Psalm 78 recounts the history of Israel. As one would expect, it describes the mighty works of God on behalf of His people. But it includes something else as well—the many spiritual failures of preceding generations.

When we teach our children, we should include both positive and negative examples. We do our children a disservice when we present an unbalanced, unfair view of the previous generation. If we deny past mistakes, we perpetuate an unwillingness to share personal weaknesses and struggles. We need to present the "good old days" honestly as a time when people struggled with sin, as they do today.

Our present lives contain a mixture of spiritual victory and failure. If we share both aspects of our spiritual journey with the next generation, we can give them valuable tools to use in their own walk with God. Don't revel in your failures, but don't hide them either. This open approach can bridge some of the generational gaps which often develop in families and churches.

Final Thought: Present the past honestly to encourage your children's relationship with God.

The Taunt of the Wicked

Psalm 79:12

"And render unto our neighbours sevenfold into their bosom their reproach, wherewith they have reproached thee, O Lord."

The world generally has little respect for believers. In media, Christians are often depicted as hypocrites, fanatics, or fools. Elements of our faith are made the material for jokes and mockery. Some people mock out of a misunderstanding, while others antagonize purely out of hatred.

While we may take these things personally, God states that such attacks on His people actually target God Himself. He takes upon Himself the affront of His children. The mocker is like a bully in the schoolyard unaware that his victim's father stands only feet away ready to intervene. When God brings the final destruction upon this age, He does so because of its rebellion against God and for the mistreatment of His saints (Rev. 19:1–2).

Asaph, understanding that the great Shepherd feels the suffering of His sheep (v. 13), calls upon God to defend His name. If people reproach God, they must anticipate the consequences of God's judgment. And God's justice will never fail.

Final Thought: God feels your suffering and gives you comfort and patience.

The Need for Restoration

Psalm 80:3

"Turn us again, O God, and cause thy face to shine; and we shall be saved."

Israel's cycle of sin and restoration portrays the struggles of believers. Israel in the Book of Judges grew comfortable with sin every time they had peace. God could not allow His people to continue in this sinful process, knowing it would lead to their destruction. In love, He allowed enemies to conquer and enslave His people until they repented and turned back to Him. Similarly, we tend to depend on God less in times of ease. God allows us to experience the consequences of our self-dependence so that we will turn again to Him.

What does restoration look like for a Christian? The joy of our salvation returns—we return to living by faith. As we humble ourselves before God, we find His welcoming arms—like those of the prodigal's father—waiting for us (v. 19). There is no condemnation, only forgiveness, as God delivers us from our guilty status. We recognize our need for salvation, not only for our soul, but also for our daily life as long as we live in the flesh and in a sinful world.

Final Thought: Quickly return to God, and He will restore you.

The Disaster of Dissatisfaction

Psalm 81:10

"I am the LORD thy God, which brought thee out of the land of Egypt: open thy mouth wide, and I will fill it."

Have you ever marveled at how repeatedly Israel turned away God? Psalm 81 begins with a celebration of God, Israel's strength. The writer calls for songs, joyful shouts (v. 1), and festive music (v. 2). The celebration turns into a feast to remember God's goodness and provision (v. 3).

The people praise God for delivering them from slavery and removing their heavy burdens (v. 6). Yet, after God provided for them time after time, the people failed to trust God when they ran out of water (Ps. 81:7; Exo. 17:1–7).

In the Law, God commanded the people not to trust other gods, but to trust Him only. If they would seek Him, He promised to defeat their enemies (v. 14), protect them (v. 15), and feed them with the finest foods (v. 16).

In spite of these commands, verses 11 and 12 reveal Israel's sin—they rejected God to find satisfaction elsewhere. They didn't listen to Him, so God allowed them to pursue their own destruction.

As Christians, we also have received precious promises from God. God desires us to depend solely on Him. Let us learn from Israel's error.

Final Thought: Seek satisfaction only in God, and He will provide.

Defend Those in Need

Psalm 82:3

"Defend the poor and fatherless: do justice to the afflicted and needy."

In our fallen world, sin always corrupts and opposes God's justice. But in this psalm, God declares both His intent and His ability to execute justice despite opposition.

As Christians, we are representatives of God to our world. We glorify God and reveal His character through our acts of love, mercy, and justice. God—by His commands and His example—compels us to help those who are weak, needy, and unprotected. By rejecting the worldly practice of exploitation and using others, we testify to God's sacrificial love.

But we must do more than simply refrain from exploiting those in need. We must work to deliver them from the oppression of the wicked and give them help. This desire appears in our response to needs after natural disasters. It also has evidenced itself in many mission works that established schools, hospitals, and orphanages as outgrowths of God's love in the gospel.

Physical aid helps to relieve suffering, but it is limited. All people will eventually die (v. 7), so we must give them spiritual aid—the gospel—as well, to benefit their eternal soul. God offers salvation through Christ to all who will believe. This is our greatest message of mercy from God.

Final Thought: Glorify God with justice and mercy.

Failure Evangelism

Psalm 83:16

"Fill their faces with shame; that they may seek thy name, O LORD."

In the Bible, we see the wicked constantly scheming against God and His children. Though they may seem to experience occasional, short-lived success, they will ultimately feel shame as God frustrates their plans.

Yet God demonstrates love even in this response to the wicked. He intends for their frequent failure to turn their eyes to heaven—that they would recognize the authority and power of the God who continually ruins their schemes. God frustrates them in order to reach them.

In light of God's plan, how should believers respond to the wicked? First, we must show grace and humility in God's victory. We can do much harm if we malign the failures of the unsaved. While we oppose evil, we should not mock the wicked when they are down. Second, we should watch for an opportunity to share the gospel when unbelievers fail. A gracious word and testimony of God's love can go a long way at those moments. Not everyone will turn to God, but some may.

Final Thought: Use God's victory as an opportunity to show love and share the gospel.

The Joy of Dwelling with God

Psalm 84:2

"My soul longeth, yea, even fainteth for the courts of the LORD: my heart and my flesh crieth out for the living God."

Do you have a favorite place that you enjoy visiting? Does a special place give you feelings of peace and joy when you think about it? As a young person, I enjoyed climbing the hills near my home. On a hilltop, I could sit in silence and stare out over the Ohio River winding through the Appalachian foothills. Even today, thinking of that place settles my mind and heart.

David sought a refuge of peace as well. As king, he continually handled matters of business, politics, and war. His days could easily fill with bickering leaders, disgruntled citizens, and threats from foreign powers. In the middle of such turmoil, David longed for the peace and fellowship he found in God's presence.

For David, visiting the courts of God meant a trip to the Tabernacle. Today, as living temples of God, we can enjoy the fellowship of God's presence continually. In our hectic lives, do we take time to enjoy that presence? Do we get alone with God?

Final Thought: You can find joy and solace in the presence of your heavenly Father.

The God Who Revives His People

Psalm 85:6

"Wilt thou not revive us again: that thy people may rejoice in thee?"

As part of living in a dying world, our sin destroys our spiritual lives with apathy and decay. As a result, we constantly need revival. God sent Christ, not simply to give us life, but to give abundant life (John 10:10). We fall short of that abundance when we allow sin to rot our relationship with God.

We experience revival when God restores our hearts and brings us back to Himself. We must be willing to allow God's work in our hearts, because we can never accomplish a revival in our own strength. Notice God's work in revival. He forgives us and covers our sin (v. 2). He replaces His wrath (v. 3) with favor (v. 1) and mercy (v. 7). He speaks words of peace (v. 8). He shows us His steadfast love (v. 10). And He produces righteousness and truth in us (v. 11). When we surrender to God, He transforms us and gives abundant life.

Not only does God produce change, but He also gives us a responsibility. He cautions us not to turn back to our sin, rebelling against Him (v. 8). We cannot expect God to produce change if we resist Him. We are foolish to seek death when God offers us life.

Final Thought: Surrender to God's work of revival.

A Prayer of Confidence in God

Psalm 86:5

"For thou, Lord, art good, and ready to forgive; and plenteous in mercy unto all them that call upon thee."

Nothing in life can steal a confidence inspired by a relationship with God. People and institutions fail us, and we regularly fail ourselves. But God has never failed. Throughout the rise and fall of history, God stands sovereignly unmoved.

Many of David's trials challenged his confidence, but he saw God work through them all. During his escape from Saul, David witnessed God's provision and protection. In the promise of kingship, David saw God's power and faithfulness. Even David's sin and failures taught him God's forgiveness and faithful love.

David developed a great confidence in God by his faith in God's character. Only God could hear and preserve His people (vv. 1–2). God shows mercy and rejoices in His servants (vv. 3–4). God is quick to forgive all that call on Him (v. 5).

God's unchangeable character gives us confidence. Imagine trying to serve a god who always changes. We could never know how he would respond to us or if he would even choose to listen. But our God never changes His Word or His character. This is the confidence of the righteous.

Final Thought: Only God can give you true confidence.

The Response of the Confident Saint

Psalm 86:8

"Among the gods there is none like unto thee, O Lord; neither are there any works like unto thy works."

Yesterday, we read of the confidence we can have in God, a confidence based in His unchanging nature. Today, we will look at three ways confidence in God impacts our lives. How will our day be different because we believe in God's unwavering love toward us?

First, we will depend on God for help (v. 7). We can identify someone's source of confidence by observing what he or she does in time of need. When we trust God, we will naturally pray to Him in our troubles. He isn't a last resort; He is the constant focus of our hearts and prayers.

Second, we will walk in God's truth (v. 11). We desire God's truth because we know it contains life and joy. We want to walk in the paths of His righteousness, found in His Word. Reading His Word and meditation become regular parts of our day.

Third, we will praise and glorify Him (v. 12). We praise God when we communicate our confidence in Him with our words and actions. We show that God is worthy of all people's trust and worship.

Final Thought: How does your life display your confidence in God?

The City of God

Psalm 87:2

"The LORD loveth the gates of Zion more than all the dwellings of Jacob."

By the fifth century, many Christians regarded Rome as God's city upon Earth. Over several centuries, Roman emperors had transformed this city into the financial, political, and religious center of the known world. No greater city could be imagined. People expected Rome to stand forever, but their confidence was crushed when a Visigoth army pillaged the city in AD 410.

The sack of Rome prompted Augustine of Hippo (a city in Algeria, North Africa) to write his classic work, The City of God. In it, Augustine argued that no earthly city could lay claim to the title, "City of God." God's city has not yet appeared on Earth. It will arrive at the Last Judgment, and all God's people will gather there in joy and peace forever.

In the Old Testament, Jerusalem—which the psalmist refers to as Mount Zion—represented the promise of a future, heavenly Jerusalem. The New Jerusalem will perfectly fulfill its title—"City of God's Peace." God loves this city and has prepared it for His Son (Rev. 21:1–2).

Today, nearly all people know of earthly Jerusalem and its conflicts. But in the last days, everyone will declare the beauty of the New Jerusalem and the blessedness of its citizens.

Final Thought: Despite the conflict present in your earthly life, God will reign in peace in the New Jerusalem.

A Prayer in Despair

Psalm 88:14

"LORD, why castest thou off my soul? Why hidest thou thy face from me?"

Without the hope offered in the following chapter, this psalm would leave us in the depth of despair. The psalmist, Heman, recounts his sufferings, which he endured from his youth (v. 15). He wept day and night over his troubles (v. 1). He felt like one of the dead (vv. 3–5). He had no comfort from others, for his friends and family had forsaken him (vv. 8, 18).

In this pit of despair, one glimmer of hope remained. Five times in this chronicle of sorrow, Heman cries out in prayer to God. Circumstances have overshadowed his faith but not extinguished it. His heart yet hopes that God will listen and respond.

We sometimes find ourselves in places of darkness. Suffering, lonely, and powerless, we despair of the weariness of life. But we pray nonetheless, because God alone remains our hope, and we desperately need Him to hear.

Final Thought: In life's darkest moments, cry out to God in faith.

God's Enduring Faithfulness

Psalm 89:2

"For I have said, Mercy shall be built up for ever: thy faithfulness shalt thou establish in the very heavens."

Psalm 89 ends the third division of the Book of Psalms like the sun dawning after a starless night. In the previous psalm, Heman despaired of his life and the promise of God. But this psalm provides an answer to that despair. In this psalm, the psalmist Ethan sings of God's mercy, love, and faithfulness.

Ethan rests his hope in the promises of God (vv. 3–4). God works in heaven and Earth, fulfilling the promises He makes to His saints. He created all (v. 11), and none of His creation can resist the power of the Creator (v. 13). Justice fills His throne, and He executes perfect judgment (v. 14).

The psalmist also finds confidence in his relationship with God (v. 26). God is his Father, full of love and mercy. The Lord is his God, deserving worship and praise. And God is the rock of salvation, securing and assuring his deliverance. This same God provides these things to us, as well. He loves us, faithfully pursues us, and draws us to Him. The enemies of God oppose us. Our own sin causes us to stumble. But God never forsakes His own, because He is faithful forever.

Final Thought: God, right now, faithfully shows you His mercy and love.

Our Everlasting God

Psalm 90:2

"Before the mountains were brought forth, or ever thou hadst formed the earth and the world, even from everlasting to everlasting, thou art God."

We lack the ability to understand the eternal. Everything around us decays and wastes away. We constantly replace worn clothing, repair broken cars, and renew expired memberships. The great cities of the past have become the ruins of today. Our physical world doesn't give us a reference point for eternity.

But our eternal God transcends the physical world. The writer of this psalm attempts to illustrate that eternality with two pictures. He presents the God who is not bound by creation or by time.

God exists apart from His creation (v. 2). Though mountains seem to stand forever, they had a beginning when God formed them, and one day they will have an end. But God has neither beginning nor end. God existed before anything we see in the world began.

God also exists outside of time (v. 4). For us, time dominates our lives—our schedules, our bodies, and our understanding. But God is not bound by time. One day and a thousand years are the same to Him.

Final Thought: Our God is from everlasting to everlasting.

Relating to an Eternal God

Psalm 90:12

"So teach us to number our days, that we may apply our hearts unto wisdom."

God's eternality can easily overwhelm our limited understanding. How can we—with our short life spans and daily struggles—ever relate to an eternal God? We could not, unless God had pursued us Himself. God uses our temporal nature to emphasize His eternality.

Our lives pass quickly (v. 10). Many of us labor for as much as seventy to eighty years, but we still eventually pass away. The entrance of sin into the world brought death to humankind. If not for God's sustaining mercy, life would cease all together (Col. 1:17).

What does this teach us as God's people? First, we must recognize our brevity in order to pursue wisdom (v. 12). We can seek the eternal wisdom of God in this life. Second, we find joy in seeing God's plans, not ours, accomplished (v. 16). Our plans fade away with us, but God's works endure. Finally, we prayerfully look to God to enable our efforts for His glory (v. 17). When our labors and ministries are touched by the eternal, they receive new purpose in an otherwise purposeless world.

Final Thought: Commit your life and labor to the eternal Lord.

True Health and Prosperity

Psalm 91:2

"I will say of the LORD, He is my refuge and my fortress: my God; in him will I trust."

God promises help in our time of need, but some people claim that God will also give believers perfect health and prosperity. Their error lies in focusing on the deliverance rather than the Deliverer. Our hope as believers rests in the God we trust, not in the outcomes He promises.

When we abide in God, we receive the blessing of security under His wings. All of our trials—war, loss, illness—must pass through God before they can reach us. He allows only those trials that will ultimately help us.

We find protection in God only when we seek Him. God shows faithfulness to those who love Him and desire to know Him (v. 14). A love for the world brings destruction, but a love for God brings deliverance.

God does not promise a trouble-free life, but He promises to be with us during our troubles (v. 15). We receive deliverance and glory at the end of trials, whether our trials end in this life or when we pass into eternity.

Final Thought: God protects you when you seek Him.

Great Works Beyond Understanding

Psalm 92:5

"O LORD, how great are thy works! and thy thoughts are very deep."

We find pleasure in seeing a mystery unraveled. We love hearing mystery stories, whether from Sherlock Holmes or the evening news. We respect those who can solve riddles, from the detective to the archeologist. Often, the mysteries with seemingly no answer ignite our curiosity the most.

In Psalm 92, the psalmist introduces one of the greatest mysteries—the deep plans and mighty works of God. How can God use all the choices of our free wills to accomplish His plans? How can one Being weave together so many loose ends and conflicting schemes? How can God triumph when so many fight against Him?

We see only glimpses of the answer to this great mystery. We see generations of the wicked fade away as cut grass (v. 7). We see God repeatedly assert His power over people's plans. We have enough evidence to sing His praise and to trust His will (v. 15).

Final Thought: God's works in your life are rooted in His unsearchable wisdom and power.

A Lasting Legacy

Psalm 92:13

"Those that be planted in the house of the LORD shall flourish in the courts of our God."

Because our life on Earth is short, we can only create a lasting legacy by uniting ourselves to the eternal God. God intends the righteous to flourish (v. 12). This is one reason He gave us His Word. As we learn of God, seek Him, and walk in His ways, our paths are established. We find success—wisdom in our actions—in God (Josh. 1:7–8).

Today's psalm echoes Psalm 1, where the psalmist uses the imagery of a tree to illustrate our prosperity in Christ. But this tree—instead of being planted by rivers of water—puts down roots in the courts of God's house (v. 13). Here, watered by the Word, it bears fruit well into old age (v. 14). The passage of time brings greater spiritual health and flourishing.

God righteously works in the lives of His people. He never rewards a life of love and service with barrenness. Certainly we experience dry seasons, but God desires our fruitfulness.

Final Thought: Root yourself in the courts of the Lord for enduring fruit.

God Enthroned Above the Waves

Psalm 93:4

"The LORD on high is mightier than the noise of many waters, yea, than the mighty waves of the sea."

Psalm 93 paints a masterful picture of God's greatness. God enters the scene as a great King wearing robes of majesty and strength (v. 1). Just as God establishes the earth so that no person can move it, so He establishes His throne on the broader foundation of His eternal character (v. 2).

His throne stands forever unshaken in spite of efforts—both human and demonic—to remove it (v. 3). History records the tidal waves of human efforts to beat God's reign or shout down its King. And this satanic rebellion continues even today. If it were possible to overthrow God, people would have done so by now.

But His throne stands. The King sits untroubled by the waves and floods (v. 4). His words sound out clearly over the thundering of many waters. God remains sovereign in spite of the waves. The palace of the Lord adorned with holiness—separate from all the houses of this world's rulers. Enemies come and go, but the Lord remains forever.

Final Thought: Never let the noise of the waves distract you from the majesty of the Lord.

The Blessing of Chastening

Psalm 94:12

"Blessed is the man whom thou chastenest, O LORD, and teachest him out of thy law."

Growing up on a farm, there were some places my parents made off limits for my sister and me. We couldn't go into the room where the fertilizer was stored. We couldn't wander into the woods alone. And we certainly couldn't play on the farm equipment. My parents wanted to keep us away from danger.

The Psalms repeatedly teach two truths about the path of the wicked. First, this path always leads to destruction. Second, this path is the prominent path in this world, and it draws many toward it. In the Sermon on the Mount, Jesus taught that few enter the narrow gate of life, but many enter the wide gate of destruction (Matt. 7:13–14).

Because we're naturally drawn to the path of destruction, we receive God's special grace in the form of chastening and discipline. Through chastening, God works in our lives to shepherd us away from sin and back to the way of righteousness. The process, though sometimes unpleasant, preserves us from a far greater fate. God's chastening prunes us so that we can bear the fruits of righteousness.

God never forsakes His children. He continues to teach us His law (v. 12). He draws us into His rest as the doom of the wicked approaches (v. 13). He puts us in a place of blessing, for He rewards the righteous (v. 15). He protects us from the iniquity and wickedness that destroys those on the path to destruction.

Final Thought: Thank the Lord for His chastening.

Praise and Worship

Psalm 95:1

"O come, let us sing unto the LORD: let us make a joyful noise to the rock of our salvation."

The parallel activities of praise and worship summarize the ideal life of a believer. In these two words, we find the purpose for our daily labors, our ministry, and even our eating and drinking (1 Cor. 10:31). All we do should give praise or worship to God. Psalm 95 introduces these two concepts with a call to believers—"O come" (vv. 1, 6).

When we praise God, we publicly declare His goodness and greatness. While ultimately directed to God, our praise communicates God's character and works to others. We declare that He is our strong salvation (v. 1). We reflect the joy that only He can give (v. 2). We proclaim that He alone is God (v. 3). We speak of the beauty and might of His creation (vv. 4–5).

When we worship God, we acknowledge our place under His authority and our joyful submission to Him. He is our Maker, our Shepherd, and our Deliverer (vv. 6–7). Our only correct response is to hear His word and submit (vv. 7–8).

When we fail to praise and worship, we miss out on the blessings of God. We resist God by choosing our ways rather than His (v. 9). We go astray following our own heart's desires (v. 10). And ultimately we miss out on the rest that only God provides (v. 11).

Final Thought: Make your life a practice of praise and worship.

A World of Idols

Psalm 96:5

"For all the gods of the nations are idols: but the LORD made the heavens."

Satan continually tries to deceive us, sometimes with outright falsehood and slander against God, and sometimes in subtler ways. One of his subtle attacks is to promote religious pluralism, thereby lowering God to the level of the gods and idols of the world. In the Old Testament, Israel frequently practiced pluralism when they adopted the gods of the pagan nations around them, usually after intermarriage with the Canaanites.

Because of sin, people grow increasingly acceptant of spirituality without religiosity. People advocate tolerance for all forms of spirituality, frowning on any claims of absolute truth. You may have your God as long as you acknowledge the gods of others.

In Psalm 96, God calls us to challenge pluralism with praise. We sing His greatness (vv. 1–2), tell about His offer of salvation (v. 2), and declare His glory and works (v. 3). We combat pluralism, not by attacking false gods, but by exalting the one, true God. By exalting Him to His rightful place, we declare all other gods to be false. He alone possesses true strength and majesty (v. 6). He alone deserves our worship and every glory ascribed to His name.

Final Thought: Let your praise for the one true God challenge the world's idolatry.

Those That Love God

Psalm 97:12

"Rejoice in the LORD, ye righteous; and give thanks at the remembrance of his holiness."

The proof of a person's cooking comes when you finally eat the meal. The evidence of a great builder lies in the soundness of the building. And the test of our love appears in our actions towards the object of that love.

Psalm 97 divides nicely into three stanzas. Verses 1–5 demonstrate the power and righteousness that God exercises from His throne. Verses 6–9 reveal the results of His reign upon Earth. Idolaters fall into shame, but the worshippers of God rejoice. The final stanza shows the response of those who love God.

Those who love God hate evil (v. 10). The words "love" and "hate" in the Bible are usually volitional rather than emotional. The psalmist states that loving God—that is choosing Him as your highest treasure—means that we will necessarily reject evil. Christ taught this principle in the Sermon on the Mount, stating that we cannot serve and love two masters—God and our desire for personal gain (Matt. 6:24). When we love God, we will not allow anything to take priority over Him in our lives.

Those who love God also rejoice in Him and in His righteousness (v. 12). We promote God's rule and righteousness because we find true joy in Him alone. Without His righteousness, we have no righteousness. Again, Christ echoed this truth in His Sermon on the Mount, telling us to seek first God's kingdom and righteousness. True love seeks God and rejoices in what it finds.

Final Thought: In light of God's greatness, pursue Him above all else.

Oh Sing to the Lord

Psalm 98:1

"O sing unto the LORD a new song; for he hath done marvelous things: his right hand, and his holy arm, hath gotten him the victory."

Throughout the Bible, God emphasizes our praise and worship to Him. The central book of our Bible, Psalms, is filled with songs of praise to God.

The inspiration for our songs comes from God's work of salvation. God has delivered us from the path and destination of the wicked. Because of this deliverance, we have a "new song" that the unredeemed cannot sing. The Holy Spirit teaches us a melody foreign to those still enthralled by the world.

By His creation, God has given us the means to express our new song. He has given us musical instruments (vv. 5–6). He has given us voices (vv. 4–5). Even those who lack musical skill can laugh, shout, or cheer in response to His great works (v. 4).

Even the earth praises God in its own way. The seas roar, and the rivers clap their hands in praise. The hills sing for joy (v. 8). Deserts and cities lift their voices (Isa. 42:11). When all the earth praises God—from the height of the heavens to the lowest deeps (Isa. 42:23)—how can we refrain from joining in?

Final Thought: Have you sung your new song lately?

Tremble Before the Lord

Psalm 99:1

"The LORD reigneth; let the people tremble: he sitteth between the cherubims; let the earth be moved."

Some Christians exhibit a dangerous tendency to corrupt the biblical image of God as Father. They portray God as a permissive, indulgent, and easily manipulated parent who hangs on His child's every whim while ignoring their misbehavior. Psalm 99 presents a stark contrast to this teaching as it presents God's terrible might, justice, and power.

God is exalted in position and power. He sits enthroned among His servants, the cherubim (v. 1). Just one of these servants once slaughtered an entire army and another time killed all the firstborn of Egypt. God sits high above all people (v. 2). We can only approach His footstool (v. 5).

Even the greatest leaders of Israel submitted to God and honored Him (v. 6). In their interactions with God in the wilderness, Moses and Aaron often fell on their faces before God. Samuel, a prophet and judge of Israel, submitted to God as a young child (1 Sam. 3:10). God spoke to His people in the wilderness, thundering forth from the dark clouds covering Mt. Sinai. The people trembled at the voice but soon forgot their fear and sinned against God. Though God forgave them, He still allowed them to experience the consequences of their sin (v. 8). The only right response was to honor and reverence God.

Final Thought: God is your loving Father, but He also deserves your reverence.

The Offering of Thanksgiving

Psalm 100:4

"Enter into his gates with thanksgiving, and into his courts with praise: be thankful unto him, and bless his name."

When friends or relatives invite us over for dinner, my wife invariably asks, "What can we bring?" We bring a gift to our host or hostess as a sign of love, friendship, and appreciation. Many cultures have practiced this custom since the beginning of time.

In Psalm 100, God invites us, not only into His house, but into His very presence (v. 2). We enter into His gates and come into the courts of His house (v. 4). You and I have never received a greater invitation.

But what do we bring our Host on such an occasion? God deserves our greatest and most precious possessions—which already belong to Him by right—but that is not what He asks. What does our wealth matter to a God who owns the cattle of a thousand hills? No, when we enter God's gates, He wants us to enter with thanksgiving and praise. That is the gift He desires.

Final Thought: When you come to God, bring thanks for all His goodness to you.

A Prepared House

Psalm 101:2

"I will behave myself wisely in a perfect way. O when wilt thou come unto me? I will walk within my house with a perfect heart."

My wife endeavors to keep our house within an hour of being guest-ready. (It took only 15 minutes before we had kids.) This means that with a little tidying and wiping down surfaces, we can entertain all comers.

In Psalm 101, David writes about keeping our spiritual house in order in anticipation of fellowship with God (v. 2). We do this not to impress God, but rather to show humility and reverence. David begins by evaluating his own walk. He seeks wisdom and a pure heart in all that he does (v. 2). He guards his eyes to avoid anything that would turn him toward wickedness (v. 3).

David also evaluates the company he will keep. He allows no place for the wicked or perverse (v. 4), who are full of slander and pride (v. 5). Those who tell lies and love falsehood are equally shut out (v. 7). Instead, David fills his house with the faithful and those who pursue a right walk with God (v. 6).

In this psalm, God calls us to consider our own spiritual house. Do we continually prepare it for divine visits, or do we neglect its care, feeling embarrassed before God?

Final Thought: Part of loving God is keeping your spiritual house in order.

A Prayer of the Afflicted

Psalm 102:24

"I said, O my God, take me not away in the midst of my days: thy years are throughout all generations."

Psalm 102 records the prayer of a person overwhelmed with an affliction. It opens with the echo of the psalmist's tortured cry. He lists the multitude of suffering he had endured:

- He suffers burning pain (v. 3).
- He is so heartsick that he forgets to eat (v. 4).
- He feels alone (v. 6).
- He can't sleep (v. 7).
- His enemies mock him (v. 8).
- He weeps constantly (v. 9).

In the face of such suffering, the psalmist encourages himself by reflecting on God's eternality and mercy (vv. 12–13). God will not forsake His people or ignore the prayers of the desperate (vv. 16–17). This confidence lends us hope even in our deepest despair.

Why then did the psalmist record his affliction? He recorded it so that fellow sufferers in generations to come would look to God in their affliction and praise Him (v. 18). Remember that God hears (vv. 19–20). Remember that God alone lives eternally (vv. 24b–27). Remember that God establishes the generations of His children forever (v. 28).

Final Thought: Pour out your sorrows to God and remember that He hears.

Remembering God's Benefits

Psalm 103:2

"Bless the LORD, O my soul, and forget not all his benefits."

Do you ever find yourself doubting God's goodness in hard times? In dark times we can easily forget the light. To remedy this, we must meditate on the ways God has blessed us in the past.

Consider all the blessings that God pours out on His people. Some are personal and specific blessings, meeting our unique needs. Other blessings are general, shared by all of God's children. David lists many of these shared blessings in Psalm 103. Let's look at some of them:

- God forgives our sins (v. 3).
- God heals our diseases—some now, and all in heaven (v. 3).
- God redeems us from the destruction we deserve (v. 4).
- God makes us His royal children and heirs to His love and mercy (v. 4).
- God provides us with good things to renew our strength (v. 5).
- God defends the cause of the oppressed (v. 6).
- God revealed and recorded His works through His Word (v. 7).
- God deals with us in His mercy rather than in His anger (vv. 8–11).
- God removes our sins as far as the East is from the West (v. 12).
- God shows pity and fatherly compassion (v. 13–18).

As God's children, we share in all these blessings. Do not forget the many blessings we have received from our heavenly Father and King.

Final Thought: The faithful God gives eternal blessings to His people.

Remembering God's Greatness

Psalm 104:1

"Bless the LORD, O my soul. O LORD my God, thou art very great; thou art clothed with honour and majesty."

As if the psalmist knew our tendency to doubt God's promises, he follows yesterday's psalm with the one we are considering today. Psalm 103 lists God's blessings, and Psalm 104 lists the aspects of God's greatness. God's greatness gives substance and certainty to His promised blessings. These amazing acts and attributes ought to inspire us to bless and praise our God. Let's look at the descriptions of God's greatness in this psalm:

- God clothes Himself with shining honor and majesty (vv. 1–2).
- God uses all creation to serve and promote His purpose (vv. 3–4).
- God created the waters and the land, setting their boundaries (vv. 5–9).
- God provides perfectly for the needs of His creation (vv. 10–18).
- God established unchanging times and seasons (vv. 19–23).
- God displays amazing variety and creativity across His creation (vv. 24–26).
- God sustains His creation (vv. 27–30).

All of God's creation offers us a portrait of God's greatness. Every work of nature reveals His power. The perfect balance displays His wisdom. And daily sustenance reveals His mercy.

Final Thought: God created the world to reveal His greatness.

Joy in Seeking God

Psalm 105:3

"Glory ye in his holy name: let the heart of them rejoice that seek the LORD."

As a young person growing up on a produce farm, I quickly learned never to complain about boredom. There was always plenty of work for a bored child. But even without expressing it, I still felt bored. Looking back, I realize the boredom sprang from my activities. One can only read so many novels, play so many video games, or watch so much TV before losing interest in the novelty of these activities.

But those who truly seek God do not find such limitation in their pursuits. Spend an hour in thanksgiving, and more remains for which to express gratitude. Spend a day singing songs to God, and more songs will swell in your heart. Spend a week relying on His strength, and you will desire even more of His power. Spend a lifetime praising Him, and enough praises will remain to fill eternity.

Our heart will not find lasting satisfaction in this life, but the heart that seeks after God will find no end to the joy of pursing Him.

Final Thought: Find true joy in seeking after God.

How Do You Use Your Deliverance?

Psalm 106:43

"Many times did he deliver them; but they provoked him with their counsel, and were brought low for their iniquity."

Humanly speaking, Psalm 106 presents a discouraging picture. The psalmist recounts the repeated failures of God's people to remember God's deliverance and provision. The psalmist begins by narrating seven rebellions of the people in just the first 40 years after the Exodus. Then he summarizes the rest of Israel's history. They failed to obey God by driving out those who rejected Him. They mingled with the heathen people and worshipped their false gods. Finally, God sent His people back into bondage so they would return to Him.

What a sad response to God's deliverance. Israel could have enjoyed the blessings of God's freedom but insisted on their own way, ending up in captivity. Paul warns believers of the same danger. We have liberty in Christ, but we must guard against returning to bondage to the Law or the flesh (Gal. 5:1, 13–14). God has delivered us with an even greater deliverance than the Exodus. Isaac Watts captured this right response to deliverance in one of his lesser-known hymns:

> *Lord, thou hast heard thy servant cry*
> *And rescued from the grave;*
> *Now shall he live; and none can die,*
> *If God resolve to save.*

> *Thy praise, more constant than before,*
> *Shall fill his daily breath;*
> *Thy hand, that hath chastised him sore,*
> *Defends him still from death.*

Final Thought: Your freedom in Christ is a great gift. Use it wisely.

A Return to Praise

Psalm 107:8

"Oh that men would praise the Lord for his goodness, and for his wonderful works to the children of men!"

Psalm 107 begins the final section of the Book of Psalms. The last section ended with a recounting of Israel's failure and hope that God would hear His people's cry (Ps. 106:44) and save them (106:47). Psalm 107 opens with praise for God's goodness in remembering and restoring His people. This psalm's tone of praise and rejoicing provides the theme for the rest of this book.

Perhaps you can relate to this theme of praise. You may have experienced a period of turning from God, even after He saved you. Like the prodigal son, you may have left the Father behind to seek joy and satisfaction in this world. But sin never satisfies, and its pleasures only last for a short time. The psalmist pictures this time of neglecting God as being lost in the wilderness. He dwelt alone with none to comfort him (v. 4a). He found no city of refuge from the dangers of wild beasts or robbers (v. 4b). He suffered hunger and thirst to the point of near death (v. 5).

If you currently relate to this spiritual experience, repent and return to God. Like the prodigal's father, God waits for you. Or perhaps you have returned to the Father and found His arms open wide. If so, you have reason to rejoice in the goodness of God.

Final Thought: God restores the repentant saint and delights in his or her renewed praise.

Assured Victory

"Through God we shall do valiantly: for he it is that shall tread down our enemies."

In every struggle and battle, we can confidently trust our steadfast God. We can demonstrate our assurance in word and action, knowing that He will work with mercy and power. God will deliver His beloved and exalt Himself among the nations.

The heart of this psalm reflects David's confidence in God. He describes the lands and regions within the Promised Land as if they already belonged to him. He harbored no doubt that God would fulfill His promise. God always completes the works He begins.

God has begun a work in your life as well. When He redeemed you, He began a lifelong project of conforming you to the image of His Son. You, like all of us, have much in your life that hinders this transformation. Opposition persists even as our desire for sanctification grows. Some days it may even feel that the flesh has the upper hand. But be assured that God has never been defeated, and He will vanquish the enemies of your sanctification.

Final Thought: God's triumph is certain, and He will complete the work of salvation in your life.

Turning Cursing into Blessing

Psalm 109:28

"Let them curse, but bless thou: when they arise, let them be ashamed; but let thy servant rejoice."

Psalm 109 records another of David's prayers against his enemies. These enemies had received love from David (v. 4), but they responded with lies (v. 2). Under such attack, David calls upon God to reward the wicked according to their sin. He asks God to destroy their name from the earth (v. 15).

As David draws toward the end of his prayer, his tone changes. He knows God will judge the wicked, but rather than ending his prayer with a desire for judgment, he begins to pray for himself. He asks God to show mercy and love to him (v. 21). And he wants God to work in such a way that others will see God's work and glorify His name. He petitions God to take the curses of the wicked and turn them to blessing.

Even today your love for God and others may be misunderstood or misrepresented. People may say unkind and untrue things about you. But our God is still in the business of turning curses into blessings for His people.

Final Thought: God has good planned for you. Leave the cursing of the wicked in His hands.

Christ's Eternal Reign

Psalm 110:1

"The LORD said unto my Lord, Sit thou at my right hand, until I make thine enemies thy footstool."

Have you ever considered the unfathomable mind of God? Psalm 110 gives us a rare glimpse into the conversation among the members of the Trinity. Here Jehovah, the Father, speaks to the Messiah, His Son. The conversation involves the ultimate fulfillment of Messiah's lordship over all things. The Father tells the Son to wait at the right hand until all enemies are overthrown.

Over and again, the Bible speaks of this ongoing conflict. Christ already reigns as King, but opposition abounds. Both spiritual forces and powerful people rail against Christ's reign. They would throw off His laws and claim His dominion for themselves.

But the Father promises an end to all opposition. Today, He preserves Christ's reign over His enemies (v. 2). Christ's kingdom expands around the globe. And one day, the Father will end all rebellion. He will strike kings (v. 5). He will judge the rebellious nations and slay the evil (v. 6a). He will topple powerful people who stood against the Son (v. 6b). None shall be left to oppose God.

Final Thought: Rest assured that Christ's kingdom is coming and will come.

Christ's Eternal Priesthood

Psalm 110:4

"The LORD hath sworn, and will not repent, Thou art a priest for ever after the order of Melchizedek."

Yesterday we saw the promise of Christ's eternal kingdom. He will reign as King forever, and He will vanquish all enemies. But what if you choose to submit to Him? How will you fare in this final judgment?

The people of Christ are also being prepared for this eternal kingdom. But instead of conquering them, God prepares them through sanctification. He clothes them with holiness, so that they may rejoice in the day of Christ's triumph (v. 3). As He overthrows the enemies, God prepares the righteous for eternity.

Thus Christ, the conqueror of the wicked, lives as an everlasting Priest to His people (v. 4). He intercedes for us, serving as the only mediator between God and humankind. He prays for our provision. He prays that His righteousness might be perfected in our lives. So shall we be prepared for His eternal reign as our King and Priest.

Final Thought: Christ, your High Priest, is preparing you for eternity.

The Song of the Upright

Psalm 111:1

"Praise ye the LORD. I will praise the LORD with my whole heart, in the assembly of the upright, and in the congregation."

Over and again the psalms remind us that God's people naturally sing His praises. When we gather together, we give thanks for all His mighty works (v. 1). We remember the providential working of God in our lives and history and praise Him for it (v. 2). Having discovered His fingerprints on our life, we marvel at the glory and majesty of those providences.

The psalmist records a few of his personal meditations on God's good works.

- The Lord provides food (v. 5).
- The Lord promises the inheritance of all nations (v. 6).
- The Lord sends redemption (v. 9).
- The Lord keeps His covenant forever (v. 9).

Notice the timeless nature of God's work. He has worked in the past, providing and preserving. He works today through similar provision as He advances the cause of His kingdom. His works will one day fulfill His covenant, and He will bring all things under the Son for the good of His people. No wonder the psalmist concludes by declaring, "His praise endures forever!"

Final Thought: There is no end of God's praiseworthy works.

The Blessing of the Upright

Psalm 112:9

"He hath dispersed, he hath given to the poor; his righteousness endureth for ever; his horn shall be exalted with honour."

Are you among the upright described in Psalms 111 and 112? How would you know, and what would you anticipate as the fruit of uprightness?

The upright—those who obey God—reflect God's blessing in their life to others. They delight gladly in God's commands (v. 1). They are gracious, merciful, and righteous (v. 4). They live a life of immoveable faith in God (vv. 7–8). The Lord has worked in these yielded hearts, crafting a tool with which to bless others.

The upright blesses his own household. He raises and trains his children to carry on righteousness in spiritual might (v. 2). His possessions increase even as he uses them to bless others (v. 3). His five talents, thus invested, quickly produce ten.

The upright also blesses those beyond his household. He shows kindness and wisely executes his business for the good of his clients, students, or customers (v. 5). He gives to the poor and distributes God's provisions freely and joyously (v. 9). His neighbors are thankful to know him. The only ones grieved are the wicked. But God preserves the upright from even these enemies.

Final Thought: God wants to work in you so that you may be a blessing to others.

Who Is Like the Lord?

Psalm 113:5

"Who is like unto the LORD our God, who dwelleth on high?"

Among other reasons, the Bible calls on us to praise God for His uniqueness. This praise spreads through all time and space (vv. 2–3) because none in Earth or heaven can compare to Him (v. 4).

None can approach to God's exalted position (vv. 5–6). God dwells on high in inaccessible light. The earth cannot bear God's glory, but neither can heaven. The sinless angels still cover their faces in His presence. Even a perfect creation cannot compare to the exalted Creator.

None can comprehend His plan and power (vv. 7–8). At His will, the poor are exalted. He sets up whom He desires and determines the rulers of the nations. No one can oppose His plans.

None can match the joy He provides His people (v. 9). He works impossible blessings for His people, as when He caused Sarah, Hannah, and the Shulamite woman to bear children. He designed David to rise from shepherd boy to Israel's greatest king. He restored Job's losses with a twofold blessing. He brought Joseph from a pit to a palace. Who but God could do such improbable things?

Final Thought: No god of human invention can match the wonders of your God.

A God Who Makes the Earth Quake

Psalm 114:7

"Tremble, thou earth, at the presence of the Lord, at the presence of the God of Jacob."

God displayed amazing power in the Exodus and its aftermath. Because we are so familiar with this story, we can become numb to the true magnitude of its miracles. But for Israel, this served as a defining historical moment. God made Israel great through Abraham, but He adopted them as His own nation through the Exodus.

Three great miracles showed the might of God in establishing His people. First, God divided the Red Sea to deliver His people from Egypt (v. 3). He made a dry path through waters deep enough to later destroy the horses, chariots, and soldiers of Pharaoh.

Second, God shook the mountain of Sinai (v. 4). This miracle often gets overshadowed by the Ten Commandments. Before the Law was given, the people trembled as God appeared in a thick cloud and shook the mountain.

Third, God provided water in the desert (v. 8). Out of dry, hard rock, God brought forth life-sustaining water. He kept the people from certain death and by doing so, assured them of His loving care.

In these three miracles, the psalmist is reassured that God has adopted Israel as His own. They are the people of an all-mighty God. Let us all tremble in His presence.

Final Thought: You are the child of an all-mighty God.

Hollow Gods

Psalm 115:3

"But our God is in the heavens: he hath done whatsoever he hath pleased."

As a child I would receive chocolate bunnies for Easter. Opening the wrapper, I would often be disappointed to discover that the bunny was hollow. The chocolate was only a quarter-inch thick. The rest was empty air. Psalm 115 tells us that mankind's idols are similarly deceptive. They look good, but on closer examination, they are only empty promises—hollow gods.

These hollow gods are created. The craftsmen do the best they can, but the idols have several flaws (vv. 4–7).

- They cannot speak—they give no truth, wisdom, or revelation.
- They cannot see—they are blind to their worshippers' needs.
- They cannot hear—they are deaf to prayers.
- They cannot smell—they cannot receive the savor of their worshippers' sacrifices.
- They cannot work—they lack any power to act for good or ill.
- They cannot walk—they are motionless and bound to their place.

And the greatest tragedy of idolatry is not the hollow nature of these gods. The greatest tragedy comes upon those that make and trust in idols. These people become hollow just like the gods they worship (v. 8). They become weak, blind, and deaf, unable to defend themselves in the day of trial and judgment.

Final Thought: Humankind has never created a god with any true power.

A God Above All Idols

Psalm 115:11

"Ye that fear the LORD, trust in the LORD: he is their help and their shield."

All of us have experienced that person who freely criticizes his opponents. He claims to be faster, smarter, and stronger than everyone else on the court. But often such boasting proves hollow once the actual game begins. God, however, never makes an empty boast.

After describing the impotency of human-made idols, the psalmist praises God's power. In verses 9–11, the psalmist emphasizes three times that people must trust in the Lord. God alone provides help and a shield to those who trust in Him.

In contrast to humankind's gods, our God acts on behalf of His worshippers:

- God remembers and blesses His people (vv. 12–13).
- God causes His people to flourish (vv. 14–15).
- God does whatever He pleases from His throne in heaven (v. 3).

God reigns over the heavens, and He rules over the world and its fleeting cares. People construct gods of gold and silver or gods of power, wealth, and entertainment. These hollow gods provide only false, momentary security or pleasure. While many people content themselves with what they can make of this world, we seek something greater. We seek the true God of all.

Final Thought: Bless forever the true God of the heavens.

The Other Side of Darkness

Psalm 116:8

"For thou hast delivered my soul from death, mine eyes from tears, and my feet from falling."

Today's psalm records the experience of one whose path ran into a deep, dark valley of sorrow and despair. The psalmist had endured a great trial of physical and emotional anguish. He felt surrounded by death and sorrow (v. 3). He was brought very low by this unnamed struggle (v. 6). His life had consisted of tears, stumbling, and feelings of death (v. 8). Even the help of others seemed useless and untrustworthy (v. 11).

All of us pass through this valley—none are exempt. Some must travel deeper or more often than others. Though the misery seems endless, our path will eventually lead back to joy and peace. The psalmist emerged from this valley and rediscovered joy, and he relates how others may find it as well.

First, the psalmist prayed (vv. 1–2). In depression's valley, prayer seems to have a hollow echo. But God is listening. No one has ever escaped the valley without calling on Him repeatedly. Nearly a dozen times, the psalmist cries out for God in this psalm.

Second, the psalmist resettled his heart and hope on God (v. 7). He reminded himself of the blessing of resting and waiting on God. It is hard to look up in the valley, but we must. Only God can see our entire path, and we must trust His knowledge and purpose in our blindness.

Finally, he reconnected with the people of God in serving the Lord (vv. 9, 14, 18–19). Having re-centered on the Lord, the psalmist once more joins in the worship and service of the Lord. Those people he rejected in verse 11 now become his companions (vv. 14, 18–19). The valley was long, but at the other end he found rest in God and rejoicing with God's people.

Final Thought: Look to God in the valley of despair. He is a steadfast hope.

Short and Simple

Psalm 117:1

"O praise the LORD, all ye nations: praise him, all ye people."

Psalm 117 is the shortest chapter in Scripture. Its brevity highlights the simplicity of its message—the correct vocation of all people, and the two reasons we should be busy about this work.

God created all nations and people to praise Him. Sin prevents all people from fulfilling this calling, but the calling remains. You exercise your created purpose when you praise the Lord in life, labor, and service.

Why does God deserve such universal praise? First, He shows steadfast love and kindness toward humankind. Believers experience this in a special, familial way, but all people enjoy the general blessings of God. Second, the Lord remains eternally faithful to His Word and nature. No one else can claim unmarred unfaithfulness. God never changes. He is faithful and always will be. Praise the Lord!

Final Thought: Your ultimate task is to praise the Lord.

God's Gift of Freedom

Psalm 118:5

"I called upon the LORD in distress: the LORD answered me, and set me in a large place."

Psalm 118 speaks of three deliverances that God gives to His people. Today we will look at the first two. Tomorrow we will look at the greatest deliverance God provides.

Verse 5 speaks of the Lord delivering us from "distress." This word literally means "tightness" or "a tight place." Have you ever found life circumstances pressing you until you felt suffocated or trapped? In such times, we can call on God. He can set us in large places where we enjoy the joy of freely following and worshipping Him.

Verses 6–13 proclaim God's power to deliver us from oppression. With God as our helper, we have no reason to fear the power of our enemies (v. 6). The wicked and godless can attack, surround, and press us, but God is stronger than they. He gives us the ability to endure and triumph. He is our strength and song, and He has become our salvation.

Final Thought: God gives you freedom in the trials and conflicts of life.

The Open Gates of Righteousness

Psalm 118:19

"Open to me the gates of righteousness: I will go into them, and I will praise the LORD."

Last time, we meditated on God's deliverance of His people in this world. He alone is more powerful than those who oppose us. But we need deliverance not only from trials and conflicts, but from our sin and guilt, as well. We need Someone to open for us the gates of righteousness (v. 19–20).

We know that we could never open these gates on our own. From birth we are as far from righteousness as the East is from the West. Our greatest need is righteousness, but it is the very thing we completely lack. God must make a way for our righteousness (v. 21).

Looking to God for righteousness, we see the gate opened in a most startling way. The way is so unusual and unexpected that most people reject it (v. 22). God opens the way to righteousness with His rejected Son, and He delights to do so.

And when we enter at that gate, God greets us with blessing (v. 25). First, He saves us from the world, our own sin, and future destruction. Second, He brings true success to our labors. Truly His love for us endures forever.

Final Thought: In Christ, God opened the gates to righteousness for you.

A Song About a Book

Psalm 119:1

"Blessed are the undefiled in the way, who walk in the law of the LORD."

Only one psalm separates the shortest chapter of Scripture from the longest. Psalm 119, the longest chapter with 176 verses, nearly doubles Numbers 7, which comes in a distant second with 89 verses. And what is the topic of the longest chapter and song in Scripture? This song discusses a Book.

Psalm 119 details the value of God's Word and how we, as His children, should relate to it. An acrostic, the psalm alphabetically and systematically records the author's life living with the Book. It speaks of such blessings as protection from sin (vv. 10–11), delight (v. 35), liberty (v. 45), wisdom (v. 48), guidance (v. 105), and many more. The Bible stands as the chief source of our knowledge of God. Therefore, to know God, we must meditate in His Word all the time.

The psalm also addresses those times when we struggle in our relationship with God. At times when all seems like dust (v. 25) and sorrow (v. 28), God's Word can enlarge our heart (v. 32). The Word provides comfort in our afflictions (vv. 49–52). It brings correction when we turn from God's path (v. 67).

God, in this psalm, testifies to the power and preeminence of His Word. A believer who forsakes this source of fellowship and cleansing will soon find himself or herself struggling in life and spirit.

Final Thought: God's Word is a precious gift to His people.

The Word and Our Way

Psalm 119:15

"I will meditate in thy precepts, and have respect unto thy ways."

We all need maps. I remember many trips while growing up where we would unfold a huge map, or leaf through the well-worn road atlas searching for the route to our next destination. Now those maps are digital, carried around in mobile devices. These maps guide us in our travels and keep us from straying from our intended path.

God's Word serves a similar purpose for His people. We live as foreigners in this world, traveling its challenging paths. God has given us commands to help us on life's journey. In the Word we behold God, but we also see how He wants us to walk in the way of righteousness. He has not left us to grope along the path on our own.

The Bible is our only guide for faith and practice. We know it teaches what to believe, but we are tempted at times to look elsewhere for guidance on how to live. Friends, family, and culture all give their opinion on how to best live in the world. God may use these things, but the greatest tool we have to navigate this life remains His Word.

Isaac Watts captured some of this in his hymn, "I Love the Volumes of Thy Word":

I love the volume of thy word;
What light and joy these leaves afford,
To souls benighted and distressed,
Thy precepts guide my doubtful way,
Thy fear forbids my feet to stray,
Thy promise leads my heart to rest.

Final Thought: Order your steps by the path laid out in the Word.

Cleansing by the Word

Psalm 119:133

"Order my steps in thy word: and let not any iniquity have dominion over me."

Last time, we saw that God's Word guides us in the way of righteousness. Psalm 119 also teaches that the Word guards us from drifting into iniquity. We need both guidance and protection if we are to survive life's journey.

Imagine traveling along the road if you had only positive instructions and no warnings. Life with no red lights or stop signs may sound preferable, but it would bring confusion, injury, and frustration. Consider even simple warning signs, such as "Bump," or as critical as, "Bridge out ahead." Such signs force us to adjust our speed or even our direction, but we are grateful for their warning.

Likewise God's Word issues warnings about this life. These warnings confront us with change—even painful change—but God intends them for our good. He knows the danger of a wrong path, and He aims to protect us from a life enslaved to sin.

Isaac Watts continued yesterday's hymn by addressing the warnings of God's Word:

> *Thy threatenings wake my slumbering eyes,*
> *And warn me where my danger lies;*
> *But 'tis thy blessed gospel, Lord,*
> *That makes my guilty conscience clean,*
> *Converts my soul, subdues my sin,*
> *And gives a free and large reward.*

Final Thought: Thank the Lord for both the guiding and guarding work of His Word.

They Call for War

Psalm 120:7

"I am for peace: but when I speak, they are for war."

We live in a world of conflicts and the lies that create them. James states that we war because of our conflicting sinful desires (James 4:1–2). Solomon blames pride (Prov. 13:10). In today's passage, the psalmist points to another cause of conflict—lies and deceitful words (v. 2).

Lying destroys the potential for peace. It works by destroying trust, the basis of peace and harmony. So many peace treaties fail because they attempt to reconcile two parties that distrust one another. Each party wants the other to be trustworthy but does not demonstrate its own trustworthiness.

Peace requires truth. This is why Paul calls on believers to speak the truth in love for the sake of unity (Eph. 4:15). Lying creates conflict because it harms others. The psalmist compares falsehoods to flaming arrows that pierce others and spread destruction (v. 4). One lie leads to another, then another. They spread like wildfire. Soon there are so many lies that even the liar isn't certain of what is true. Such confusion inevitably leads to conflict.

Final Thought: Speak truth and seek friends that minister truth to you.

The Lord Our Keeper

Psalm 121:3

"He will not suffer thy foot to be moved: he that keepeth thee will not slumber."

Why do we equip our homes with locks, watchdogs, and security systems? We secure our homes for safety when we are away or asleep. Even if we cannot personally watch over our homes, we use devices and animals that stay on guard.

But how do we ensure our own safety? How do we defend ourselves from the evils and troubles of this world? The only true answer is to look to the Lord, the maker of heaven and Earth (v. 2). What does the Lord do on behalf of those who trust in Him?

- He grants stability (v. 3).

- He never rests or fails to watch over us (vv. 3–4).

- He protects us in the daily hardships we face (vv. 5–6).

- He preserves us in our troubles (v. 7a).

- He keeps our souls from death (v. 7b).

- He guards and guides our going out and coming in (v. 8).

The eternal vigilance of our loving, faithful Father protects us every day.

Final Thought: You can confidently commit your life to God's keeping.

Fellowship in the House of the Lord

Psalm 122:1

"I was glad when they said unto me, Let us go into the house of the LORD."

Psalm 122 records the joy of the Jews' annual pilgrimage to Jerusalem. The Law required God's people to gather regularly at the Temple in the Jewish capital. God established these gatherings to fortify and display the unity of the people in love and worship for God.

The psalmist, recognizing the importance of these gatherings, calls for others to join in praying for the peace of Jerusalem (v. 6). He prays for peace and prosperity within the city so that God's people may gather for worship (vv. 7–8). Without these gatherings, the people of God would lose something of vital importance (v. 8).

Today, we can still pray for the peace of Jerusalem, but this psalm also invites us to pray for our own freedom to gather and worship. If we have such freedom, we can thank God and pray for those who defend our liberty. And above all, we must pray that God will use the gatherings of His people for His glory.

Final Thought: Praise God for the fellowship we have with other believers.

Keeping Our Eyes on God

Psalm 123:1

"Unto thee lift I up mine eyes, O thou that dwellest in the heavens."

So much of life's journey depends upon where our attention is focused. Focus influences direction, but even more, it impacts the way we experience our journey. The psalmist here pictures our need to focus on the Lord the way male and female servants focused upon their master or mistress. In a culture of servanthood, the master provided the only source of blessing. His or her goodwill was the only hope of the servant. So must our eyes look only to God as our source of good.

Why is this focus so important? Because the world has only contempt for the pursuits and aspirations of the followers of God (vv. 3–4). In the face of such contempt, we need the mercies of the Lord. We can endure this world's scorn when we focus our eyes above.

Final Thought: Keep your eyes focused on the Lord to find joy along your path.

God Alone Is Our Help

Psalm 124:8

"Our help is in the name of the LORD, who made heaven and earth."

God's people never stand in their own strength. History shows that every attempt to do so has ended in defeat, death, and slavery. God intentionally chooses the weak things of the world so that they depend on Him, and therefore give Him all the glory of victory.

The Book of Judges contains multiple instances that demonstrate this truth. The people of Israel rejected God to do whatever was right in their own eyes. God then removed His hand of protection, allowing enemies to capture and enslave Israel. Finally, recognizing their own weakness, Israel cried out in repentance for God's help. God responded with a deliverance for which only He could receive the credit.

Believers today face the same challenge that Israel did. Will we look to ourselves for strength and deliverance in this life, or will we look in faith to God? That choice will determine much of the outcome of our lives.

The psalmist pictures our plight like a bird ensnared by the fowler. The bird could never escape, but God comes along and breaks the snare. God provides deliverance from sin and its doom. He has broken the snare in Jesus Christ.

Final Thought: You will find your only help in the Lord.

Made Like a Mountain

Psalm 125:1

"They that trust in the LORD shall be as mount Zion, which cannot be removed, but abideth for ever."

Mount Zion, the hill upon which Jerusalem was built, posed a daunting defense against enemy attack. Three major valleys border Zion on the east, west, and south—the Kidron Valley, the Tyropoeon Valley, and the Valley of Himmon. Beyond those valleys, three additional mounts provided additional defense—the Mount of Olives, Mount Moriah (Temple Mount), and the Western Ridge. Combined, these provided a natural fortress for God's city.

To the psalmist and his fellow Israelites, this topography served as a visible reminder of God's defense of His people. Just as surely as God defended against physical enemies, He would defend against the wicked. And God's defense gives peace to His people.

Even today, we find peace as we rest in God's protection. Faith removes fear and assures us of the ultimate triumph of righteousness. Trust in the Lord and abide in Him forever.

Final Thought: You can fully trust God, your defense.

Joy After Sorrow

Psalm 126:5

"They that sow in tears shall reap in joy."

Like the children of Israel, we often find ourselves in valleys of our own making. Israel's history abounds with national sin leading to captivity. Similarly, our own lives reveal the sorrow and suffering resulting from our sins. Having turned our backs to God, we find ourselves in self-made pits of despair.

While Israel reflects our problem, it also reveals the solution to our misery. Israel didn't put on a stiff upper lip or make light of their suffering. No, they wept and sorrowed over the results of their sin. They allowed that sorrow to drive them back to God. They went forth, sowing seeds of repentance and obedience, and they reaped a harvest of joy.

When we find ourselves in the same sorrow of sin, we also must weep. We cry out because of our sin and the pain it has brought to us. But we need not stay there. We can and must confess our sins, repenting of our disobedience. We then arise like the prodigal son and return to the Father, ready to obey His will and serve Him. In God's welcome embrace, we find joy, laughter, and rejoicing.

Final Thought: The way of repentance and return will always lead you to rejoicing.

Beware of Vain Effort

Psalm 127:1

"Except the LORD build the house, they labour in vain that build it: except the LORD keep the city, the watchman waketh but in vain."

We lead busy lives. We work, we try to spend quality time with our family, and we seek to serve God through ministry. Yet a danger lurks within all this busyness. We can easily rely on self-effort. And self-effort never produces spiritual fruit.

The psalmist—likely David writing to Solomon—warns against three common areas in which we often rely on self-effort. First, we often labor in our own strength (v. 1a). Whether teaching, building a house, or running a company, our work is something we do day in and day out. Familiarity with the tasks tempts us to believe we can accomplish our goals in our own strength.

Second, we believe we can secure ourselves through self-effort and sufficient planning (v 1b). If we have enough insurance, a big enough nest egg, and a solid 10-year plan, we believe everything will be fine.

Third, we feel secure when we've worried enough (v. 2). We lie awake at night or wake thinking for the twentieth time about some past action or future task. We feel that running over it one more time will give us the perfect insight for the next step or decision.

Hard work, precautions, and even intense thought are not bad. But when we rely on these things, we are preparing for failure. Except the Lord work and defends us, all our efforts will be frustrated. But true rest comes when we place all things in His hands.

Final Thought: Commit all your labors and plans to the Lord.

God's Work Spans Generations

Psalm 127:4

"As arrows are in the hand of a mighty man; so are children of the youth."

Last time, we saw that laboring in our own efforts, instead of depending on God's enabling power, ultimately proves ineffective. One reason for this is that our lives are brief. In spite of our gifts, skill, and effort, few of us are given more than forty or fifty years of productive labor. Yet God is not constrained by time, because His plans extend across millennia. So how will His great work be accomplished when people lead such short lives?

God accomplishes His plan by spanning the generations of humankind. God prepares a Joshua to replace a Moses. He sends out twelve to continue the work of Christ. He commissions us all to go to the world with the gospel. One generation could never accomplish all God has planned.

This truth emphasizes the importance of ministering to children. Whether you have children of your own or God provides ministry opportunities in other ways, take time to pass on the truth and knowledge of God. God will use the next generation to fulfill His will.

To illustrate this truth, the psalmist uses the imagery of arrows in the hands of a master archer (v. 4). These arrows represent the children God has graciously placed in your life (v. 3). As you minister to them and they grow up, God launches them into other service for Him—service that you could never have accomplished. Ministry to youth is a multiplication ministry.

Final Thought: Children are the instruments of God's future plans. How are you influencing them for the Lord?

Blessings of Fearing the Lord

Psalm 128:1

"Blessed is every one that feareth the LORD; that walketh in his ways."

The fear of the Lord brings blessing. This truth echoes throughout the Bible, especially in the wisdom literature—that is, the poetic books. The fear of the Lord is a reverence for God that results in obedience to His Word. God assures us that no other way to blessing exists.

The fear of the Lord blesses our labors when we obey Him (v. 2). We enjoy the fruits of those labors because we see them as God's gifts. He provides for our needs and many of our desires, as well.

The fear of the Lord also brings blessings to our family life (v. 3). It promotes a healthy, fruitful marriage relationship, and it gives wisdom for raising children. Our family reflects godliness and encourages mutual spiritual growth.

These blessings then overflow to society at large. We see and contribute to the prosperity of God's people (v. 5). We also see this blessing passed on generationally in our own family (v. 6). Blessed is the church when it is full of such people.

Final Thought: The fear of the Lord is the only way of blessing.

The Wicked Shall Never Triumph

Psalm 129:4

"The LORD is righteous: he hath cut asunder the cords of the wicked."

The wicked perpetually seek to defeat God's people (vv. 1–2). They attack the Word of God and even challenge God's existence. They attack through many avenues as they hurl their might against the saints.

Yet their prolonged battle reveals that God has not allowed the wicked to succeed. Again and again they are turned back. But they return to attack again from another angle. Even when they succeed in oppressing the righteous for a time, God breaks the cords of their power (v. 4).

The wicked appear strong in this life, but God sees them in a different light. To God, the wicked are like plants that take root in a clogged gutter (v. 6). The weeds spring up quickly, but they find no room for growth. The heat of summer withers them, leaving the plant dry and brittle. They pass away in disgrace and fruitlessness. Both their power and their praise are short lived (v. 8).

Final Thought: Without God's blessing, the wicked can never succeed.

The Hope of Forgiveness

Psalm 130:4

"But there is forgiveness with thee, that thou mayest be feared."

We desperately need the assurance of God's forgiveness. Imagine, for just a moment, the Christian life without divine forgiveness. How long could we maintain our walk in righteousness? Could we last even an hour if God ceased to offer forgiveness for our sins and failures?

But we have no such fear. All our sin lies buried under Christ's blood. God does not mark down all our sin against us. If He did, our hope would vanish forever (v. 3). No book of your sins or replay of your failures awaits you in heaven. Our redemption is complete—all is forgiven (vv. 7–8).

This complete forgiveness and our complete dependence upon it should motivate our reverence for the Lord. We recognize how desperately we need His promise in Christ to remember our sins no more. We know that the slightest break in that promise would mean our eternal separation from God. We abjectly cling to this promise. And in His faithfulness, our hope is assured.

Final Thought: Praise God with confidence that He has forgiven your sins and will continue to forgive them.

Quieted Before God

Psalm 131:1

"Lord, my heart is not haughty, nor mine eyes lofty: neither do I exercise myself in great matters, or in things too high for me."

Most people have a driving urge to understand the how's and why's of life. God created us with inquisitive minds and the ability to grow in our knowledge. But this ability has its limits, produced by the effects of sin and our nature as created beings. There are things our mind simply cannot understand.

The danger comes when we refuse to accept this limitation. Our fear or pride prompts us to demand an answer to all of life's mysteries. We want God to explain everything to us. We insist that God answer us.

Instead of this turmoil and toiling, God calls us to the peace that accompanies a confidence in God. When we truly believe God's wisdom, love, and power, we can press on without all the answers. Like a child who receives the care from parents in ways she can't fully understand, we rest in our heavenly Father (v. 2). Certainly He has proven Himself worthy of our hope.

Final Thought: Let God be God and trust Him when you don't fully understand.

The Reign of David's Son

Psalm 132:11

"The LORD hath sworn in truth unto David; he will not turn from it; Of the fruit of thy body will I set upon thy throne."

History records the rise and fall of many dynasties. Of the thousands of families and clans who rose to power, only a half dozen held power for over one thousand years. Most maintained their place for much shorter periods. They come, and they go.

David recognized the brevity of human rule. He had taken the throne from Saul the Benjamite, though some of Saul's descendants yet lived. David had every reason to expect that his own dynasty would also someday end. But God had other plans for David.

God gave David an incredible promise—that David's reign would mark the beginning of an unending line (2 Sam. 7:8–16). One of David's descendants would sit upon the throne of God's people forever. God sustained David's line through the centuries until the promised King was born. Jesus Christ lived a perfect life, died, and rose again. And when He ascended on high, He sat down on the throne of God's kingdom forever.

Final Thought: You are a citizen of God's promised eternal kingdom.

Unity, the Blessing of God

Psalm 133:1

"Behold, how good and how pleasant it is for brethren to dwell together in unity!"

Before the fall, all creation existed in a harmonious unity. Every creature lived in perfect, perpetual worship of God. This harmony reflected the unity and fellowship within the Triune God who had created it. When sin entered the world, however, unity shattered. People were separated from God, from creation, and from other people. Sin replaced open unity with walls of pride, hatred, falsehood, and a hundred other sins.

But God had a plan to restore unity. Christ's sacrifice facilitated this return to God's creative purpose, and the ongoing work of the Spirit makes unity possible where it seems impossible. In a world of isolation and selfishness, unity becomes a shining evidence of God working in His people.

The psalmist illustrates God's purpose in unity with two objects—oil (v. 2) and dew (v. 3). Oil was used to anoint God's chosen leaders. These leaders had a responsibility to unite and bless God's people. Similarly, the dew of Hermon, which came as rain upon the mountains of Zion, provided for the crops needed to feed God's people. As oil and dew provided blessings, so unity provides blessing for the health and growth of God's people.

Final Thought: Pray that God would make you an ambassador for unity among His people.

Why We Gather

Psalm 134:2

"Lift up your hands in the sanctuary, and bless the LORD."

In a day of increasing communication technologies, it is easier than ever to receive biblical teaching without ever leaving your home. Online video services, audio recordings, and digital books put some of the best Bible teachers a mere tap or click away. We become tempted to seek God apart from a body of believers. We ask ourselves "Do we even need the old church on the corner?"

Psalm 134 concludes the fifteen Songs of Ascent—psalms sung as God's people made a pilgrimage to the Temple in Jerusalem. Imagine the interruption and inconvenience of making three pilgrimages each year to the capital of Israel. Yet this was God's command for the good of His people. God has always intended His people to gather together, demonstrating the unity we discussed previously.

But what did the people do when they had gathered together? They went to the Lord's house and lifted up their hands in praise to God. He was the destination of their journey. He was the object of their pilgrimage. Today we have no temple, but we are still called to gather (Heb. 10:24–25). And the reason for our gathering remains unchanged.

Final Thought: Gathering with God's people in worship is one of your greatest privileges and obligations.

God's Mercy Is Forever

Psalm 136:1

"O give thanks unto the LORD; for he is good: for his mercy endureth for ever."

The word translated "mercy" or "steadfast love" in this psalm is the Hebrew word hesed. The word describes unconditionally, actively seeking the good of a person. This is God's attitude towards His people. The word appears twenty-six times in this psalm, followed by the word olam, meaning "always" or "eternally." Thus, this phrase indicates that God's active love toward His people has no end.

The psalmist lists several ways that God has shown this merciful love to us:

- He created a good, self-sustaining world for us (vv. 4–9).
- He delivered His people from Egypt (vv. 10–16).
- He gave the land to Israel and removed the nations that opposed them (vv. 17–22).
- He reaches out to us in our low estate (vv. 23–25).

This last point moves from the historic work of God into His present labors of love. God still reaches down to us in our weakness (v. 23). He still offers us deliverance (v. 24). He daily provides all we need for this life (v. 25). How can we do anything but give Him thanks?

Final Thought: Take some time to meditate on God's ongoing goodness to you.

Singing in a Strange Land

Psalm 137:4

"How shall we sing the LORD's song in a strange land?"

Repentance first stirs in the heart when we recognize what sin truly costs us. In Psalm 137, this realization is pictured as the captive Israelites slumped down by the river in Babylon. Their sin, which had separated them from God, had also separated them from the Promised Land and the City of David. As their captors taunted them, demanding a song (v. 3), the people wept over their loss (v. 1).

Though the Jews grieved over their sin, that realization turned their eyes back to God. They prayed for remembrance of God's former blessings. They pursued the memory of living in God's place of blessing. Jerusalem, the earthly representation of abiding with God, would be their highest joy (v. 6). The Israelites retained this memory, for after seventy years of captivity, many eagerly accepted the chance to return home.

When we sin, we also lose our intimate walk with God. Paul refers to such times as returning to the bondage of sin (Rom. 6:16). But by God's grace, we need not remain in bondage. Repent, and joyful fellowship will be restored.

Final Thought: God never allows His children to find joy apart from Him.

God Will Complete His Work

Psalm 138:8

"The LORD will perfect that which concerneth me: thy mercy, O LORD, endureth for ever: forsake not the works of thine own hands."

When God saves a person, He begins a process of transformation in that person's life. We experience this as our Christian walk, but we must never think we walk alone or in our own strength. God assures us that He walks with us, and that He is working to complete His purpose in our lives.

David found great assurance in God's promise to complete the work of salvation. David praised God publicly for the work God accomplished. He saw God working in answered prayers (v. 3). He even foresaw all the rulers of the earth acknowledging the faithfulness and power of God to keep His word to His people (vv. 4–5).

God accomplishes His great work in spite of apparent roadblocks. Though God is exalted high above humanity, He bends down to help the humble (v. 6). Though a believer's path be overwhelmed with troubles, God gives more strength to overcome them (v. 7). God will complete His work in all whom He saves.

Final Thought: God has begun a great work in you, and He will finish it (Phil. 1:6).

God Knows You Completely

Psalm 139:1

"O lord, thou hast searched me, and known me."

God knows you completely. No aspect of your life, personality, or thoughts is hidden from Him. This truth rightly terrifies those who know Him only as a righteous Judge. But for those to whom God is a loving Father, His perfect knowledge provides comfort and hope.

God knows your path (vv. 2–3). He understands the obstacles you currently face. He foresees all the trials that lie ahead. He guides and guards along that path (v. 5).

God knows your words and thoughts (vv. 2, 4). As you encourage, exhort, and teach others, God notes and uses the words of your mouth. He also notes any idle or prideful words. He discerns perfectly the thoughts behind every word that escapes your lips. He works in you to bring forth words of wisdom and healing.

God's knowledge extends back to before you were even born (vv. 13–16). God saw and recorded your life from conception, the beginning of the story He lovingly planned for you. Be assured that God has made you and shaped your life in a way that reflects His all-knowing love. His complete knowledge of us gives hope in all our struggles and endeavors.

Final Thought: Nothing about you or your struggles is a surprise to God.

God Is Present Everywhere

Psalm 139:10

"Even there shall thy hand lead me, and thy right hand shall hold me."

Have you ever wished you could be in two places at the same time? Maybe a work obligation conflicted with one of your children's sporting events or a family get-together. Maybe you just have too many errands and not enough time. These frustrations are a part of finite human life.

But God has no such limits—He is everywhere at all times. It is impossible to find any place devoid of God's presence. East and west, height and depth, all are the same to God (vv. 8–10). The deepest darkness blazes with light before God's gaze (v. 11–12). No place and no thing are hidden from His sight. God even beheld us in the womb where He worked, forming us according to His will (vv. 13–15).

God created all and watches over His creation with a steadfast gaze. God's continual presence assures us that no kindness goes unnoticed. Additionally, no wrong we receive escapes the just eyes of the righteous God. What comfort can we gain from God's constant presence! He never leaves nor forsakes His children.

Final Thought: God will never leave you.

Lord, Stop the Wicked

Psalm 140:8

"Grant not, O LORD, the desires of the wicked: further not his wicked device; lest they exalt themselves."

The wicked hate the righteous. They view God and His righteousness as hindrances to their plans. Since God cannot be defeated, they reject Him and instead attack His children.

David witnessed many attacks of the wicked. They made plans to trouble the righteous and continually stirred up strife (v. 2). They spoke with piercing, venomous words (v. 3). And they purposefully laid traps to waylay and overthrow the followers of God (v. 4–5).

Today, the wicked still oppose God. They seek to remove God from culture. They attack the righteous and seek ways to destroy labors undertaken in God's name. They mock Christianity and the gospel. They deny God and His power.

Our response, like David's, must be to pray. We pray that God would thwart the desires of the wicked. We pray that their plans would fail so that the wicked cannot glory in their wickedness. Lord, stop the wicked and exalt yourself!

George Young captures this sentiment in the fifth stanza of his hymn, "God Leads Us Along."

> *Though sorrows befall us and evils oppose,*
> *God leads His dear children along;*
> *Through grace we can conquer, defeat all our foes,*
> *God leads His dear children along.*

Final Thought: Though the wicked oppose, God will not allow them to triumph.

Priests with God

Psalm 141:2

"Let my prayer be set forth before thee as incense; and the lifting up of my hands as the evening sacrifice."

The 16th century reformers recovered, among other things, the doctrine of the priesthood of all believers. Centuries of tradition had built an ever-expanding gap between the clergy and the laity. The clergy could read and interpret Scripture, but the common church member could not. The clergy took both parts of the Lord's Supper, but the laity only received the bread. In addition, the clergy claimed the sole right to worship God. Into this unbiblical dichotomy, the Reformers brought the piercing light of Scripture.

This doctrine appears even in the Old Testament where the visible priesthood—the Levites—still existed. David was not of the priestly tribe, but in this verse he places his worship and service on par with theirs.

The Bible teaches that every believer can and must worship God. Our prayers reach God no differently than those of the most eloquent pastor. Every labor done for the Lord praises His name—in the pulpit, the classroom, the store, or the field. As priests with God, we are called to holiness, living in a way that exalts the God we worship. Our eyes remain focused on the Person of our worship.

Final Thought: As a priest, you must worship God in all that you do and say.

Tell God When You Are Overwhelmed

Psalm 142:2

"I poured out my complaint before him; I shewed before him my trouble."

Have you ever suffered troubles you felt couldn't be shared with others? Have you ever felt as though you shouldn't even bother God with them? God wants us to bring our burdens to Him. Psalm 142 records David's desperate prayer to God when David was overwhelmed (vv. 3-4) and found himself feeling very low (v. 6).

We can see first that we may come to God honestly. David didn't prepare some beautifully-worded prayer to God. He simply poured out his heart, even complaining to God (v. 2). God knows our struggles, and we can pour out our frustrations to Him. This gives God an opportunity to meet our needs and work in our hearts.

Second, God provides the only true strength when we feel overwhelmed (v. 3). We might produce temporary bursts of energy with stimulants, entertainment, or mere willpower, but lasting strength comes only as we seek the Lord and rest in Him.

Finally, God alone cares constantly for us (v. 4). Even our dearest loved ones can't care for us constantly. They have their own trials, and they also must rest. But God, who never slumbers or sleeps, watches over us with restless, unwearied care.

We serve the same God as David. And like David we can have honest communion with our God. He hears our prayers.

Final Thought: You can honestly pour out to God your troubles.

Parched

Psalm 143:6

"I stretch forth my hands unto thee: my soul thirsteth after thee, as a thirsty land."

When God created humankind in His image, part of that image included a thirst for the infinite. Dogs don't search for meaning. Fish don't ask, "Why am I here?" Hamsters never look for something bigger than themselves. Yet humankind searches for all this and more. We long for something that transcends the day to day.

Our thirst for meaning increases with age. As children, everything was new and exciting. With additional years, we lost the ability to be enthralled by grass, clouds, and butterflies. We study, watch movies, and build relationships, seeking new experiences and satisfaction. But even the greatest knowledge has limits; the excitement fades; and relationships end due to distance, loss of interest, or death. The thirst returns with renewed intensity.

All pursuits leave us parched because God alone satisfies this soul-deep thirst. We find it satisfied in meditation on His past acts of love (v. 5). Living water flows into our lives as we recognize His daily acts of loving-kindness (v. 8). And fresh hope for the future bubbles up as we see God's hand guiding us into His perfect will (v. 10) and bringing us through our troubles (v. 11). God alone is an ever-flowing well of water.

Final Thought: You will find true, lasting satisfaction only in God.

God Stoops to Us

Psalm 144:3

"LORD, what is man, that thou takest knowledge of him! or the son of man, that thou makest account of him!"

I remember when my oldest son was an infant and truly helpless. One day I saw him lying on the floor next to a toy that was just out of reach. I watched to see if he would roll over to retrieve the toy, but he simply lay there and began to cry. Feeling pity, I bent over, retrieved the toy, and returned it to his groping hands.

How often has God stooped to us in our need? David piles up descriptions of God's work on our behalf in verse 2—unchanging source of love, our fortress, our tower, our deliverer. David pauses at the overwhelming thought of the great God doing these things for weak and lowly people. He essentially asks, "Lord, why do you even pay attention to such short-lived, helpless creatures?" (vv. 3–4). The answer, of course, is that God loves His people and delights to act for their good.

As you struggle with your own smallness and weakness, remember that your loving Father stands by watching. He will bow His heavens and come down to help (v. 5). We can delight that we are children of such a God (v. 15).

Final Thought: God's presence should comfort you and give you expectation of good to come.

Passing on God's Praises

Psalm 145:4

"One generation shall praise thy works to another, and shall declare thy mighty acts."

We all leave an inheritance to the next generation. Even if you die penniless, you leave behind the impact of your words and actions. Understanding this inevitable heritage should drive you to ask, "What should I pass on?"

First, we must pass on praise of God. That praise should be daily and continual (vv. 1–2). God provides a bottomless well of praises to draw from (v. 3). If you're not sure where to start, begin by praising Him for Christ and your salvation.

Second, we must tell of God's wondrous works. Speak often of the powerful ways God has protected you (vv. 5–6). Remember and repeat the great goodness that God pours out into your life (v. 7).

Third, we must speak of the glory of God's kingdom and power (v. 11). This points our hearers to a truth yet to be fulfilled. We see God's dominion as He works through all generations (vv. 12–13), and we anticipate the consummation of that dominion in ages yet to come (v. 20). Until that day, God preserves His people for the promised future rest (vv. 14–19).

What we pass on represents the greatest investment of our lives. May we endeavor to leave a good heritage to the generations that come after us.

Final Thought: Are you passing on God's past, present, and future work to the next generation?

Our Hope Determines Our Happiness

Psalm 146:5

"Happy is he that hath the God of Jacob for his help, whose hope is in the LORD his God."

The world offers many things in which to place our confidence. We could trust great men and women of science and politics. We might hope in the money or possessions we amass. We could even place confidence in ourselves. But all these objects fail—they will one day pass away.

The Bible says that happiness comes only from placing our confidence in God. Again and again God proves Himself worthy of our hope by His actions. He created and sustains all things (v. 6). He exercises justice (v. 7a). He feeds the hungry and frees the prisoner (v. 7b). He gives healing and strength (v. 8a). He delights in righteousness (v. 8b). He guards the traveler and cares for the widow and the fatherless (v. 9).

Because of our lack of faith in God's timing, we look elsewhere for help. But a turn away from God eventually leads away from true happiness. The Lord alone is faithful and constant. He will reign forever. He will always help. He will always deserve our praise (v. 10).

Final Thought: God alone offers you a constant source of hope.

The Compassion of Our Great God

Psalm 147:3

"He healeth the broken in heart, and bindeth up their wounds."

The final five psalms all begin with the Hebrew word, Hallelujah—praise the Lord. The psalmist offers ample reasons we should praise God. He points to God's power in creation (146:6), over weather (148:8), and against His enemies (149:6–9). He praises the Lord for preserving and exalting God's people (147:2; 149:2–5). He rejoices in all God's mighty deeds (150:2).

But the most amazing praises point to the fact that this mighty God cares for His children's individual needs (147:13). The God who numbers the stars (v. 4) works to mend the broken heart of His son or daughter. He knows of your wounds and faithfully binds them up. His omnipotent hands gently reach out to comfort and console His hurting child.

Could we truly praise a god who had power but not love? Such a god might elicit fear and worship, but our hearts couldn't join in that worship. We love God because He first loved us (1 John 4:19), and that initiating love inspires true praise.

Final Thought: The parental love of God for you should inspire true praise.

God's Creation Praises Him

Psalm 148:5

"Let them praise the name of the LORD: for he commanded, and they were created."

On a recent family visit to the zoo, I marveled anew at God's glory displayed in His creation. The experience provided special wonder as I watched my two young sons revel in the sight of God's creatures.

Their favorite area within the zoo was the aviary, where dozens of tropical birds flitted through the enclosed rainforest. The birds and the flowers competed in their vibrant colors. Delicate irises poked out among cocoa and mahogany trees that held bright red and green birds in their branches. My younger son said, "Beautiful!" at least a half dozen times. My wife reminded him that we have a God who creates and loves beauty.

Later we observed two playful otters settling down for a post-swim nap. God designed these creatures with special eyes and eye muscles. The muscles actually squeeze and release the eye, reshaping it to facilitate viewing in or out of water. The wisdom of God shines forth in such design.

The day provided a visible sermon on the nature of God. Again and again, God's wisdom, power, creativity, and care manifested itself in the animals and plants we saw. The zoo provided a choir of praise unto God.

Final Thought: All of God's creation serves to bring praise to His name.

Ever-Renewed Praise

Psalm 149:1

"Praise ye the LORD. Sing unto the Lord a new song, and his praise in the congregation of saints."

God created creative people. The image of God, planted within humanity's soul, seeks ways to express creativity. Humans paint great works of art and compose heart-stirring music. We study the mysteries of Earth and the heavens. We pen eloquent poems and prose. We redesign, redecorate, and renovate our homes. Humankind constantly creates with God's creation.

God intends us to turn our creative work into tools for praise. We turn our words and labors into worship of our King. Our prayers, though perhaps not poetic, are original songs of thanksgiving and praise. Every true sermon or lesson taught comes from a heart shaping its gifts to magnify its Creator. Each kind act—even giving a cup of water in Jesus' name (Mark 9:41)—imitates our giving God.

How do you expend your creative energies? Every labor that may be done within the will of God can be done for the glory of God. Use what creativity you have received to sing a new song unto the Lord.

Final Thought: There are endless ways for you to praise an infinite God.

Joining the Song of the Ages

Psalm 150:6

"Let every thing that hath breath praise the LORD. Praise ye the LORD."

From the moment God created sound, His creatures have sung His praise. While God laid the foundation of the world, the morning stars sang together (Job 38:4–7). That song of praise continues to echo in the beauty of God's creation.

Songs punctuate the history of God's people. After crossing the Red Sea, Israel declares in verse that "the Lord is our strength and song and has become our salvation" (Exo. 15:2). The kings of Israel—Saul, David, and Solomon—sang to their God (1 Sam. 10:5-6, 1 Kings 4:32). Coming to the New Testament, we find Jesus singing with His disciples on the eve of His death (Matt. 26:30). And Paul admonishes all believers to sing (Eph. 5:19; Col. 3:16). John reveals that this song of praise continues into eternity (Rev. 5:9; 14:3).

How about you? As you journey in the Lord's path—the way of the righteous—will you join your voice with theirs? God has provided ample material to fill your song with thanksgiving—salvation, deliverance, love, mercy, fellowship, and above all, Himself. Let everything that has breath praise the Lord!

Final Thought: The people of God ought always to sing His praise. Will you?

Additional Resources

Positive Action for Christ offers many resources to help in your walk with God, encouraging you to behold His glory and grace along life's path.

The Pursuit of God by A. W. Tozer

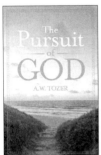

A teacher of the first order, A. W. Tozer spent his life pursuing God through his ministry and writing. In this book, Tozer declares that man can know, in a very personal way, our absolute, real, sovereign, eternal, majestic God. Like a child who takes her father's hand, we can fellowship with our God, learning from His power, grace, and love.

Christ Precious to Those That Believe by John Fawcett

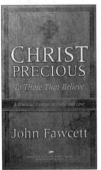

Reprinted by Positive Action, this classic work magnifies the beauty of Christ and His work. John Fawcett, an 18th century English pastor best known for his hymn "Blest Be the Tie That Binds," presents our Savior as an incomparable treasure. Without a desperate love for the Author of salvation, Fawcett argues, our obedience will remain defective. Learn to magnify Christ in your life by His grace.

Wisdom for Parents by Frank Hamrick

Anyone who has been given the privilege of raising children knows that parenting requires great wisdom. Earthly wisdom is available everywhere you look, but in this devotional, Frank Hamrick challenges you to seek God's wisdom as you reflect His love to your children.

Apples for Teachers by Frank Hamrick

Apples are a traditional gift for school-teachers, and it's our hope that this devotional will give you an "apple" a day of encouragement in your classroom ministry. Combining humor, love, and insights gained from a life of teaching, Frank Hamrick challenges you to become a wise teacher.

The Heart of the Matter by Frank Hamrick

What do you really want for the young people in your school? The purpose of a Christian school is not to teach youth how to live, but to magnify the majesty of God. Christian school teachers are not behaviorists, but cardiologists. They aim for the heart, not only to encourage academic excellence, but also to challenge students to love God and exalt His name.

For more information or to receive a catalog, please visit us at www.positiveaction.org or call (800) 688–3008.